BEHOLD AND BELIEVE

MARIAN JORDAN ELLIS

Copyright © 2022 Marian Jordan Ellis

All rights reserved.

No part of this book may be reproduced, stored in a retrieval system, or transmitted by any means, electronic, mechanical, photocopying, recording, or otherwise, without written permission from the copyright holder.

Although the author and publisher have made every effort to ensure that the information in this book was correct at press time, the author and publisher do not assume and hereby disclaim any liability to any party for any loss, damage, or disruption caused by errors or omissions, whether such errors or omissions result from negligence, accident, or any other cause.

ISBN 13: 978-1-954020-34-4 (Paperback)
ISBN 13: 978-1-954020-35-1 (Ebook)

Library of Congress Cataloging-in-Publication Data
Names: Ellis, Marian Jordan, author.
Title: Behold and Believe / Marian Jordan Ellis
Description: First Edition | Texas: TRL Press
Identifiers: LCCN 2022910953 (print)

First Edition

*FOR THIS IS THE
WILL OF MY FATHER,
THAT EVERYONE WHO BEHOLDS
THE SON AND BELIEVES
IN HIM WILL
HAVE ETERNAL LIFE,
AND I MYSELF
WILL RAISE HIM UP
ON THE LAST DAY*

— JOHN 6:40

BEHOLD AND BELIEVE

Contents

About the Author 5
Introduction 6
How to Use this Study 8
Week 1 12
Week 2 38
Week 3 64
Week 4 88
Week 5 114
Week 6 142
Week 7 170
Week 8 196
Week 9 224
Dedication 226
Acknowledgements 226
Endnotes 228

ABOUT THE AUTHOR

Marian Jordan Ellis is passionate about Jesus and helping women enjoy the victorious Christian life. She holds a Master's degree in Biblical Studies from Southwestern Baptist Theological Seminary. She is the founder of *This Redeemed Life Ministry* and serves as the Director of Women's Ministry at *Mission City Church* in San Antonio, Texas.

Marian's powerful testimony of coming to Jesus and her dynamic account of the grace of God that radically transformed her life permeate all of her writings and speaking engagements. She's experienced the abundant life in Christ and is ready to tell any ear that will listen!

Marian is the host of *This Redeemed Life Podcast*, where she equips and encourages women to love Jesus more deeply and know His power in their daily lives. In addition, she's the author of numerous books for women, including *For His Glory: Living as God's Masterpiece*, which is a verse-by-verse study of Ephesians.

In *Behold and Believe*, Marian draws upon her 20 years of teaching God's Word, combined with numerous trips to the Holy Land to study the Scriptures, to bring the Gospel of John to life for the modern women. Her love for Jesus, fascination with Biblical history, and passion for fulfilled prophecy culminate in the study you hold today.

Marian lives in San Antonio, Texas with her husband Justin. They have three children: Andrew, Brenden, and Sydney and one spoiled dog, London. You can follow Marian on Instagram or Facebook @thisredeemedlife.

INTRODUCTION

As we embark on this study of the Gospel of John, it's important to pause and consider the fact that the scriptures before us are the very words of God. These are not merely a man's ideas or recollections; what we hold is the living and breathing utterance of God (2 Timothy 3:16). In the Gospel of John, we behold the deity of Christ. We see His glory and His grace, and our hearts are moved to decide—crown Him or crucify Him?

The word "behold" proves vital for our study of the Gospel of John. Behold means to look closely, watch with thoughtfulness, and examine in order to gain understanding This greek word is where we get the English word "theatre." In this Gospel account, John invites us to behold Jesus and truly see Him for who He is— God with us. John's aim in writing this account is to put Christ's glory and deity on display so that we come to experience eternal life in Him.

Before we dive into our study, let's set the stage for this dramatic unveiling of the Son of God. According to tradition, John wrote this Gospel while living in Ephesus. He would have been one of the last surviving eyewitnesses of the Lord. While the other Gospels (Matthew, Mark, and Luke) were most likely in circulation at that time, they do not convey many of the marvelous details that John's does. The other Gospels begin with Jesus' birth or the early days of Christ's ministry, but not John's. Instead, the beloved disciple starts with Jesus' identity. He lifts our eyes to behold the One who is both Creator and Savior, both the Eternal King and the Suffering Servant.

The glorious Christ revealed in John's Gospel is majestically described by one scholar with this statement:

> *"He (Jesus) spoke, and galaxies whirled into place, stars burned the heavens, and planets began orbiting their suns—words of awesome, unlimited, unleashing power. He spoke again, and the waters and lands were filled with plants and creatures,*

running, swimming, growing, and multiplying—words of animating, breathing, pulsing life. Again he spoke, and man and woman were formed, thinking, speaking, and loving—words of personal and creative glory. Eternal, infinite, unlimited—he was, is, and always will be the Maker and Lord of all that exists.

And then he came in the flesh to a tiny spot in the universe called planet Earth—the mighty Creator becoming part of his creation, limited by time and space and susceptible to age, sickness, and death. Propelled by love, he came to rescue and save, offering forgiveness and life.

He is the Word: he is Jesus Christ."[1]

As we behold Jesus through this study of John, my goal in this study is to take you back to the Old Testament so we can comprehend the revelation of Christ in the New Testament. The Hebrew scriptures are filled with prophecies and signs that find their fulfillment in Jesus. John's Gospel is rich with this symbolism because Jesus was born and lived in a Jewish context. Therefore, it is imperative that we know the culture and promises given to the Hebrew people. Thus, in my video teaching lectures, I will focus on these Old Testament themes, while your daily homework focuses on studying John verse by verse.

By the end of our study, we will behold God's plan to redeem humanity as it unfolded from the beginning in the Garden of Eden, and how this plan culminates in Jesus Christ.

As we embark on this study, I pray for you to fall deeply in love with Jesus and that you marvel at the majesty of Christ and the magnitude of His love for you.

For His Glory,
Marian

HOW TO USE THIS STUDY

I've heard it said, "We look to Jesus to be saved, but we gaze at Jesus to be transformed." This statement has proven true in my own life, and is my earnest desire for those participating in *Behold and Believe: A Study of the Gospel of John.*

My prayer is that you would not only recognize Jesus for who He is — the King of Kings and Lord of Lords who came as your Redeemer — but my hope is that as you behold Him, you will cultivate a deeper faith, devotion, and awe of Christ. I want you to love Jesus with every fiber of your being. And I pray this love for Jesus spills over, flooding your heart, mind, soul, and spirit with the glory of God!

The format of this study is simple.

- **Begin each session by watching the teaching video.** These videos serve as an introduction to the week's lesson, enrich the homework, and highlight an Old Testament theme fulfilled in the life of Jesus Christ.
- Video teachings can be found at www.beholdandbelieve.com
- After watching the video teaching, **discussion questions** are provided for personal reflection or use with your small group.
- Then, each week in your **personal study time**, you will walk verse by verse through a few chapters of the Gospel of John. There are only **4 days of homework per week** so that you can take as much time as you need to behold His glory.

BEHOLD AND BELIEVE

Video Teaching Notes

Video teachings available for free at www.beholdandbelieve.com.

WEEK 1: BEHOLD, THE WAY

> *Jesus said, "I am the way and the truth and the life. No one comes to the Father except through me." — John 14:6*

I. The Human Condition

> *There is a God-shaped vacuum in the heart of each man which cannot be satisfied by any created thing but only by God the Creator, made known through Jesus Christ. — Blasie Pascal*

> *God made us: invented us as a man invents an engine. A car is made to run on petrol, and it would not run properly on anything else. Now God designed the human machine to run on Himself. He Himself is the fuel our spirits were designed to burn, or the food our spirits were designed to feed on. There is no other. That is why it is just no good asking God to make us happy in our own way without bothering about religion. God cannot give us a happiness and peace apart from Himself, because it is not there. — C. S. Lewis*

II. The Redemption Story

The Bible is not a collection of stories or fables; it is not a book of virtues. It's a story about how God the Father redeems us through His Son.

> *You study the Scriptures diligently because you think that in them you have eternal life. These are the very Scriptures that testify about me. — John 5:39*

III. Key Words in the Gospel of John; John 1:1–18

Logos:

Light:

Behold / Beheld:

Tabernacle:

> *And the Word became flesh and tabernacled among us. We looked upon His glory, the glory of the one and only from the Father, full of grace and truth.*
> *— John 1:14 TLV*

Glory:

IV. Behold and Become

> *And we all, with unveiled face, beholding the glory of the Lord, are being transformed into the same image from one degree of glory to another. For this comes from the Lord who is the Spirit. — 2 Corinthians 3:18*

SMALL GROUP QUESTIONS

1. The Bible explains that human beings are created by God and for a relationship with God. But when sin entered the world, the union between God and humanity was severed. Now we live with fear, insecurity, emptiness, shame, and suffering due to this broken relationship. Referring to this broken state, Saint Augustine wrote: "Thou hast made us for thyself O Lord and our heart is restless until it finds rest in thee." How are we as human beings restless?
2. In John 14:6, Jesus said, "I am the way, the truth and the life. No one comes to the Father except through Me." Jesus' words are both an invitation and a prescription for the troubled soul. What does He offer?
3. What is radical about Jesus' claim to be "the way?"
4. Marian taught five key words from the Gospel of John. Take a few minutes to define each term.
5. Read John 1:14. What does it mean that Jesus "tabernacled" among us?
6. What did you come to behold and believe about Jesus from today's teaching?

WEEK 1

Day 1: John 1:1-18

In the Gospel of John, we don't find a detailed chronology of Christ's life as recorded in Luke or Matthew. Instead, we are given a defense for the Incarnation—that God became a man. John's eyewitness testimony demonstrates that Jesus was and is "the very heaven-sent Son of God and the only source of eternal life." †

We live in the age of social media where Twitter, Instagram, Facebook, and TikTok fill our lives with images and ideas instantly captured and shared for the world to see. It's hard for us to comprehend the time in which Jesus walked on earth, when his disciples penned the Gospels. There was no such thing as "going live" on social media to share a story or post an image for those early followers of Christ. But honestly, how cool would it have been for Peter to whip out his phone and record as Jesus walked on water? Alas, that didn't happen, but we do have their eyewitness accounts of these incredible moments.

Those first eyewitnesses of His glory relied on the common method of their day to relay information—pen and parchment. In these accounts, which we call the Gospels, the followers of Jesus shared their up-close and personal moments with the One they came to worship as Christ the Lord.

> *The writers of the four Gospels have given us "snapshots" of our Lord's life on earth. Matthew wrote with his fellow Jews in mind and emphasized that Jesus of Nazareth had fulfilled the Old Testament prophecies. Mark wrote for the busy Romans. Whereas Matthew emphasized the King, Mark presented the Servant, ministering to needy people. Luke wrote his Gospel for the Greeks and introduced them to the sympathetic Son of Man. But it was given to John, the beloved disciple, to write a book for both Jews and Gentiles, presenting Jesus as the Son of God.[2]*
> — Warren Wiersbe

---

† Barton, B. B. (1993). *John* (pp. viii–ix). Wheaton, IL: Tyndale House.

WEEK 1

Throughout this study, we will encounter real people, like you and me, who came to Jesus thirsty, hungry, desperate, and burdened with great need. While he cared for their physical needs with great love, Jesus looked beyond their earthly circumstances to the deeper and more pressing need of their souls. In coming to Jesus, these people came to believe that He was indeed the Son of God, and as a result of this simple belief, they were supernaturally transformed.

What does John say is his intention in writing this Gospel in John 20:31?

John's purpose is that we might experience the eternal life that is found only in one Person, Jesus Christ. With this lofty goal in mind, let's begin the prologue (introduction) to the Gospel of John.

Read John 1:1–18. As you slowly read and meditate on each verse, note how many times "the Word" is mentioned.

Read the definition of "the Word" in the margin. What insight does this definition give you into the text?

Review John 1:1–5. What specifics do you learn about "the Word?"

John begins his Gospel with the phrase, "In the beginning." For the Jewish reader, these three powerful words would immediately connect their thoughts to Genesis, and the very first words of the Bible.

The Word

John 1:1 reads, "In the beginning was the Word." The term translated as "Word" is the word logos, in Greek meaning "word, speech, or utterance." Logos refers to divine reason or the power that puts sense into the world, making order instead of chaos. Greek philosophers sought to answer the ultimate questions of reality. They wanted to find the ultimate reality that lies behind all other things. As the ancient philosophers pondered these questions, they came up with a term to describe this ultimate reality, which was logos. The logos came to be understood as that which gave life and meaning to the universe.

> *"The light which reveals the world does not make the darkness, but it makes the darkness felt. And this is what Christ has done by his coming. He stands before the world in perfect purity, and we must feel as men could not feel before he came, the imperfection, the impurity of the world. Whether we know it or not the light which streams from Christ is ever opening the way to a clearer distinction between good and evil. His coming is judgment. The light and the darkness are not blended in him, as they are in us. The coming of Jesus into the world exposed the world's darkness."*
>
> JAMES M. BOICE

Read Genesis 1:1–3. What occurred in these verses?

Notice that God's method of creation was the spoken word. What came forth when He spoke the words, "let there be?"

According to John 1:3, what was made "through Him?"

John beautifully begins his introduction of Jesus by telling us that He, the Word, was there with God at the creation of the universe; that He IS God. Marvel at this revelation: it was through Jesus that God spoke the world into being!

Write John 1:4–5.

In verse 6, we are introduced to a new character. His name is John the Baptist. It can be a little confusing when the author's name is John, and he is speaking about someone else named John. We will talk much more about John the Baptist later; just note for now that these are two different men.

Read John 1:6–8. What was John the Baptist's primary mission?

According to verse 9, who was coming into the world?

WEEK 1

The one whom John calls "The Word" is now called the "Light." Just as light reveals, illuminates, guides the way, exposes the darkness, and unveils hidden things, the same is true of The Word.

How do you feel when in pitch-black darkness? Do you recall a time when you desperately needed to find a light or escape a dark place?

According to verses 12–13, which is the key to unlocking the entire Gospel? What rights are given to those who "receive the light?"

To "receive the Light" means to believe in Jesus. As we walk verse by verse through John's Gospel, we will discover the vital importance of the word "believe." We will note the cause-and-effect relationship that results when one believes in Jesus and behold the blindness of those who do not believe.

Read Word Study: "Believe" in margin. How is belief in Jesus more than an intellectual exercise?

Now we turn our attention to some of the most important verses in the entire Bible. Without exaggeration, I would say that throughout all of Scripture, since sin entered the world in the Garden of Eden, humanity has waited for this declaration. All the pain, brokenness, and dysfunction of humanity has led to this divine moment—the revelation of the Word of God.

Believe:
"This verb is used 78 times in the Gospel of John. It is interesting that John never uses the noun form, only the verb. Belief is not primarily an intellectual or emotional response, but basically a volitional response." Volitional means that is a choice of the will to do something with the belief. *"This Greek term is translated by three English terms: believe, trust, and faith. It is parallel to "welcome Him", and "accept Him." Salvation is free in the grace of God and the finished work of Christ, but it must be received."*[†]

[†] Utley, R. J. (1999). *The Beloved Disciple's Memoirs and Letters: The Gospel of John, I, II, and III John* (Vol. Volume 4, p. 11). Marshall, Texas: Bible Lessons International.

> "The Son of God became a man to enable men to become sons of God."
>
> C. S. LEWIS, MERE CHRISTIANITY

Read John 1:14–18 once more and answer the following:

According to verse 14, what mind-boggling event has occurred?

Pulling together all that we've discovered about "The Word", what makes this revelation that He became flesh (or human) so astounding?

Verse 14 tells us that the Word comes from the Father, "full of _____ and _____."

According to verse 16, what do we receive from His fullness?

In verse 17, John reveals the identity of the Word. He says that "the law was given through Moses" but "grace and truth" came through _____!

Now we conclude John's introduction of Jesus, the Word. We are told that Jesus brings grace and truth to the world and in Him we have life. But John concludes with one last startling statement.

Read John 1:18. What does Jesus do?

This statement brings us full circle. The purpose of a spoken word is to reveal a hidden thought. For example, I cannot know what my husband is thinking unless he reveals his thoughts through words. The same is true of God. For us to know Him, to understand His heart and to experience life in Him, He uses His Word. The Word, Jesus Christ, became flesh (a human) so that we can know God. Jesus is God revealing Himself to us.

Take a minute to marvel: "The Word became flesh and dwelt among us." Talk to God about what you learned in today's study. Use this space to express your adoration and thanksgiving.

Day 2: John 1:19-51

I love hearing stories of how people came to know and follow Jesus. In the church world, we call these "personal testimonies." My husband's testimony is one of my favorites. Justin was always what you would call a "good kid." He grew up in church, and following the rules was something he did pretty naturally—unlike me, his wife, who excelled in breaking all the rules! But that's a story for another day!

There's a powerful lesson we learn from Justin's story. Striving to be a good person and practicing religious rituals does not equal a relationship with God. Justin would tell you that he knew religion, but he did not know Jesus.

Justin was in his early thirties when life as he knew it fell apart. During the recession, he lost his job. Then a few months later, his marriage fell apart. At the same time, his mother was diagnosed with stage-4 cancer. Religion did not prepare him for this crushing season. He found himself desperate for God, for His direction, healing, and hope. This is the moment when Justin truly experienced his personal need for God's grace and encountered Christ.

I love to hear him describe this scene: On his face, crying out to God, confessing his need, Justin heard Jesus speak these simple words, "Get up and follow me." A clear command—follow Me. Rising from that place of brokenness, Justin entered a living and breathing relationship with Jesus marked by total surrender and daily dependence. Since that day, Justin has been following the One whom John describes in this Gospel.

Today we dive into the Gospel of John and hear several people share their Jesus testimonies. We begin with John the Baptist, who will testify to the religious rulers of that day about Jesus' identity and mission. Next, we will see when the very first disciples heard Jesus say, "Follow me," and how these men left everything to do just that.

Read John 1:19–28. Describe this scene in your own words.

Here we see a delegation of religious leaders from Jerusalem (priests and Levites) coming to question John the Baptist about his identity and the reason for his ministry.

What did John the Baptist say the purpose of his ministry was in verse 23?

John the Baptist is the forerunner to the Messiah (or Christ). God chose him as the announcer of the Messiah's arrival. It was common practice in that day for a king to send a "forerunner" into a region announcing the king's coming so the people of the land could prepare for his arrival. Upon hearing the news, citizens would clean

WEEK 1

the village streets, arrange festivities, and prepare the visitation. This ministry of preparation was the role John the Baptist played.

Read the Word Study: "Christ" in the margin and answer the following:

When the religious leaders ask John the Baptist if he is the Christ, what are they trying to find out?

Is the title Christ (or Messiah) an important one for Jesus to carry? Why?

One Bible scholar notes: "The Gospels portray Jesus as accepting the title and role of "Christ the Messiah." At His baptism by John, Jesus received the outpouring of the Spirit and God's mandate to begin His ministry. Jesus' baptism should be understood as His anointing to the threefold office of Prophet, Priest, and King. John himself denied being the anointed one and identified Jesus as "the Christ." Jesus' first disciples followed Him because they knew He was the Messiah.[3]

Read John 1:29–34 and answer the following:
What title does John the Baptist give Jesus in verse 29?

According to verse 31, what was the purpose of John's entire ministry?

What does John testify to having witnessed in verses 32–34?

Christ:
Many say the name Jesus Christ without realizing that the title Christ means "the Anointed One." The Greek word is "Christos", which is a translation of the Hebrew word, Messiah. Both terms come from verbs meaning "to anoint with sacred oil." In the Old Testament, Messiah was applied to prophets, priests, and kings. All of them were anointed with oil, which was the symbol that God had specifically chosen them for their respective offices. But the preeminent Anointed One would be the promised Messiah.[†]

---

† Carpenter, E. E., & Comfort, P. W. (2000). In *Holman treasury of key Bible words: 200 Greek and 200 Hebrew words defined and explained* (p. 249). Nashville, TN: Broadman & Holman Publishers.

What title does John give to Jesus in verse 34?

John's testimony is this: The Lamb of God is the Son of God. This is divine mystery revealed in the person of Jesus. In the rest of this study, we will spend a great deal of time investigating Jesus' role as the Lamb of God who takes away the sin of the world. But for our purposes now, let's look at this phrase in context of John the Baptist's testimony. When John points Jesus out to the gathered crowd, he prophesies concerning Jesus' destiny.

John the Baptist is considered the last prophet of the Old Testament. After literally hundreds of prophecies concerning the long-awaited Messiah, John stands up as the last of the prophets and declares HE IS HERE! Concerning the significance of this declaration, James Boice writes:

> *For centuries Israel had known all about the sacrificial lamb. They had learned about it first from the story of Abraham, who was the father of their nation. At God's command Abraham had been going up the mountain to sacrifice his son Isaac when Isaac had turned to him and asked, "Father, … Behold the fire and the wood, but where is the lamb?" Abraham had answered, "My son, God will provide himself a lamb for a burnt offering." And God did!*
>
> *Israel had also known about the lamb as a result of the institution of the Passover. On that occasion the blood of the lamb on the doorposts of the house was the sign for the angel of death to pass by. Moreover, they knew that daily in the services of the temple lambs and goats were sacrificed. They knew that in every instance the sacrifices meant the death of an innocent substitute in place of the one who had sinned.*[4]

Take a moment to contemplate the promise that Jesus is the Lamb that takes away the sin of the world (v.29). How do you think the original hearers would have comprehended John's declaration?

How does this truth hit your heart today?

We conclude today's study by seeing how those who heard John's testimony responded to it. As we will discover throughout this Gospel, there is always a response to Jesus. There is no neutral ground. One either believes and follows Him as Lord or turns away in unbelief.

Read John 1:35–51.

What was the response of John's disciples when they heard him declare, "Jesus is the Lamb of God" (verse 37)?

What did Andrew do after he began to follow Jesus (verses 40–41)?

Who did Andrew testify Jesus to be (verse 41)?

What did Jesus say to Peter when they first met (verse 42)?

> "There is a ripple effect to the gospel that's inevitable. There's a ripple effect to true grace. It doesn't lead us to only sit and contemplate what happened to us. It leads us to proclaim what's happened to us—and what can happen to anybody and everybody on the planet."
>
> LOUIE GIGLIO,
> FINISH THE MISSION

What does Philip testify about Jesus to his friend Nathanael in verse 45?

What simple phrase does Philip say when faced with Nathanael's doubts about Jesus (verse 46)?

After encountering Jesus personally, what was Nathanael's testimony (verse 49)?

These confessions and declarations about Jesus are wonderful, but they are only the beginning of what we will discover about Him. I love what James Boice writes concerning Nathanael's confession that Jesus is the Son of God:

> *The first chapter of John reveals Jesus in a variety of contexts and under an unusual variety of names. He is the Word, the Light, the Lamb, the Son of God, Rabbi, the Messiah, the King of Israel. These titles culminate in the confession of Nathanael who, after some initial skepticism, declares, "Rabbi, you are the Son of God; you are the King of Israel" (v. 49).*
>
> *At this point, however, Jesus answers that all the insight and experience that these confessions embody, wonderful as they are, are only a prelude to an infinite series of such experiences that lie ahead. That is, there is more to come. He therefore declares, "I tell you the truth, you shall see heaven open, and the angels of God ascending and descending on the Son of Man" (v. 51).*[5]

Friends, there is more to come! Throughout the next eight weeks, we will see Jesus and by beholding His glory, we will experience life abundantly.

Take a minute to marvel at Jesus' words: "You will see heaven open." Use this space to express your worship and praise.

Day 3: John 2:1-12

Dressed in white, with my wedding veil blowing in the wind, I walked down the aisle on a gorgeous spring day to meet my groom. With tears of joy streaming down my face, I held tightly to my father's arm as he handed me off to marry my best friend. The day I married Justin was the happiest day of my life. The photos of the day do not do justice to the elation we felt—we worshipped, we danced, we feasted, and we celebrated the goodness of God.

One word encapsulates the whole experience for me—JOY! After waiting on God for marriage for so many years and watching the Lord work in my relationship with Justin in the dating process, I came to our wedding day with a sense of being in God's perfect will and feeling the sheer pleasure of God in the marriage ceremony. After all, God is the Author and Creator of marriage. (The Bible literally begins in Genesis and ends in Revelation with a wedding celebration.) Marriage is God's idea, and He loves a good party. So, when the Lord saw fit for Justin and me to become one, I sensed I was standing on holy ground.

I love that John's Gospel begins with Jesus attending and saving (spoiler alert) a wedding ceremony. Not only do we get a glimpse of

Jesus' humanity in this story, but we also discover an important lesson about the work He came to accomplish on earth.

Read John 2:1–12.

What sights, sounds, smells, and sensations would surround a wedding feast?

How does it humanize Jesus to imagine him in this setting?

In the Jewish tradition, the wedding would take place on a Wednesday. The festivities began when the groom and his friends made their way in procession to the bride's house. This was often done at night, when there could be a spectacular torchlight parade. Next, the bride and groom went together to the groom's house, where the wedding ceremony was held. This religious ceremony was followed by the wedding feast, which typically lasted for seven days. During the feast, food and wine were supplied by the families to their guests. To run out of either implied a thoughtless or impoverished host. Running out of wine would bring dishonor upon the family name.

Read John 2:3–5

What problem does Mary bring to Jesus?

Most scholars assume that Mary and Jesus were somehow related to those hosting the wedding, which makes sense, considering that Jesus shows up with an entourage. It appears from the text that His mother has a close connection to the family and is one of the few to know that they ran out of wine. As a personal favor to the hosts who were facing tremendous shame, Mary turns to Jesus for help. Of all the wedding guests present, Mary knows Jesus better than anyone. She knows the miraculous events surrounding His birth and the promises made by the angels concerning His destiny.

Read Luke 1:26–38 to better understand Mary's perspective about Jesus:

What is Mary told about the son to whom she would give birth (verses 32–33)?

What title is given to Jesus? (verse 35)

Considering the circumstances of His birth, what do you think Mary's expectations are of Jesus?

I think all parents think their kids are special, but in Mary's case, she has valid reason for her expectation. When faced with the potential shame of the ruined wedding feast, she goes to the one person she knows is capable of a miracle.

How does Jesus respond to Mary (John 2:4)?

These words may sound a little harsh to our ears, but they did not have a harsh sound in the original language. "Woman" was a title of respect, much like our word "lady." Jesus used this same term again when he was addressing His mother from the cross as He committed her into John's safekeeping.[6] (See John 19:26)

> "The miraculous is always happening, even though we forget it or even when our faith is too small to trust God for miracles or even when we don't see the miracles occurring. God is always still at work, and God will always provide for us."
>
> LOUIE GIGLIO,
> THE COMEBACK

Jesus' response to Mary's request is actually a key to understanding the whole Gospel of John. When He says, "My hour has not yet come," He speaks of the hour of His death. He knows the minute He begins to publicly display His power through miracles, an invisible clock will begin to tick. The masses will flock to Him as word of His power spreads. As a result, the time of His crucifixion will draw closer as the jealousy of the religious authorities increases because of His popularity with the people.

Despite this reality, and fully knowing that He is going public once He performs this miracle, Jesus steps into the need of the hour.

Read John 2:5–11

What does Mary tell the servants?

What instructions does Jesus give to the servants?

What does the text indicate the water jars were typically used for (verse 6)?

A little context will help us appreciate the miracle we behold here in this text. The Old Testament Law required various ceremonial washings, but the religious leaders of that day added their own additional rules and regulations. Elaborate cleansing rituals (hand-washing ceremonies) were customary and expected. The six stone water jars mentioned in this passage were kept for the rite of purification. These rituals were religious attempts to cleanse the outer body, but they could never cleanse sin from the heart.

What similar rules do people create or practice today to cleanse the outside (behaviors) but have no or little effect on cleaning the heart?

After the servants obey Jesus' command to fill up the water jars, the miracle of transformation occurs. Supernaturally, at the word of Jesus, one substance (water) becomes a new substance (wine). This renovation of molecules is just a glimpse at the power of Jesus.

What do you think the servants feel or think as they obey Jesus' instructions and carry the first glass to the master of the feast to taste?

How does the master of the feast respond to the new wine?

I love how John wraps a bow on this joyous wedding scene with this understatement, "This, the first of his signs, Jesus did at Cana in Galilee, and manifested his glory. And his disciples believed in him" (John 2:11).

Note in verse 11: What did the miracle of transformation do? "_____" His GLORY!

The word "manifested" means to reveal or to make evident. This sign put His glory on display for all to see. Such is the case with this miracle. Water turning to wine isn't just a great card trick that Jesus performed to entertain some wedding guests and to save a family from shame. This miracle points to the reason Jesus came—

Seven Signs:
The Gospel of John is built around seven miracles that prove Jesus' identity as the Son of God. While John tells us that all the books in the world could not contain all that Jesus did, he intentionally chose to share seven specific signs. Not only do they manifest His glory and bring those around Jesus to a point of decision, but they also served to reveal something deeper about Jesus and His ministry.

to transform the human heart and to save us from the guilt and shame of sin. The fact is the human heart is sinful, and apart from God's grace, no amount of external religious cleansing can cure our condition. This is why Jesus stepped on the scene of human history: to usher in the New Covenant, which transforms us from the inside out. He does away with the old system and brings in the new one based on His life, death, and resurrection. In believing in Him, we are the water that becomes wine! Let's take a closer look at the New Covenant and how this miracle reveals Jesus' mission.

Read Jeremiah 31:31–40.

What promises does God make about the New Covenant?

How are these promises like Jesus' miracle of turning water into wine?

In the wedding at Cana, the water represents humanity's attempt to clean our sinful hearts by following rules and keeping religious rituals. Frankly, there's not enough water in the world to do that job. We need something more powerful. This is where Jesus enters our story.

While wine in the Bible was symbolic of joy, celebration, and happiness, it would soon come to represent something even more powerful—the blood of Jesus Christ.

Read 1 John 1:7–9 and Luke 22:20 and share what you learn about the blood of Christ:

Each time we take communion or celebrate the Lord's Supper in church, we remember the blood of Jesus that was poured out for the forgiveness and cleansing of our sin. This miracle points us to the greatest miracle of all—the transformation of the human heart. When we put our lives in the hands of the Master, He turns water into wine!

Take a minute to praise Jesus for His transforming power. Use this space to invite Jesus to make something new in you.

Day 4: John 2:13-25

Our wedding at my family's farm in East Texas was a dream come true. The one hitch was that there was a massive amount of work to turn a rustic horse barn into the wedding venue of my Pinterest dreams. So, I spent the day before the wedding with my bridal party, decorating my family's barn for the big day. Outdoor weddings are risky enough in April with the constant threat of rain on the radar, but add actual farm animals to the mix, and you never know what might happen.

While setting up the tent and tables for the reception, I heard a little commotion behind me. When I say "little," I should clarify. The commotion began with the sound of folding chairs being knocked around. It was quickly followed by a litany of female screams. Turning around, I saw a Longhorn steer, who usually has free range in that part of the pasture, creating his own little rodeo in the middle of my reception tent. Let's just say he caused a ruckus. Thankfully my nephew quickly stepped in to save the day, and the bridal party was able to get back to work and set up for all the festivities.

I share this story because the disturbance the Longhorn caused reminds me of the scene we behold today in the life of Christ.

I don't know your image of Jesus, but I dare say that most people are startled to see Him cause a commotion.

Read John 2:13–17.

Describe the scene in your own words.

What reason does the text give for Jesus' actions (verse 17)?

As we journey through the Gospel of John, it is important to keep in mind the author's purpose in writing. He tells us explicitly that he writes so that we might believe that Jesus is the Son of God and experience life in Him. Each scene from the life of Christ was chosen specifically to reveal Jesus' identity, mission, and heart.

In today's reading we see Jesus take up a whip and drive merchants and money changers out of the temple courts. This dramatic act reveals His' intense passion for two things—His Father's glory and the redemption of the lost.

Why does Jesus cause this commotion? The text tells us that "zeal for His Father's house consumed Him." Zeal is a word of intensity and passion. It shows us that Jesus is angry at the injustice, abuse, and degradation He sees in the temple.

Not only is He angry at the confusion, the clutter, the noise, and the smells, but primarily He is angry at the extortion and racketeering that was going on. A little context will help here. Once a year, Jewish males had to go to the temple in Jerusalem and pay a temple tax. Every male Jew was required to pay a half-shekel tax at the Passover season. Additionally, that tax could not be paid in Roman or Greek coins but had to be paid in a special temple coin. Therefore, the moneychangers are there to do the exchange. Having them available for the people was a convenience. Still, the injustice was the outrageous price being extorted for making this exchange. Sometimes, half of the value of the money being exchanged was paid to the moneychangers for their service. The temple was making huge revenues from this practice and cheating the people.

In addition, a sacrifice offered at the Passover season had to be made using an animal without blemish or imperfection. Worshippers would bring their offerings to the temple courts to be inspected before offering. Most of the time, these animals were rejected, and the people were forced to buy from the temple sellers.

This meant that the only animals that could be offered were bought from the temple herd that was kept in an open courtyard in the court of the Gentiles. These animals had already been approved by the priests. But again, a significantly inflated price was demanded. For example, a bird that could be bought outside the temple for the equivalent of 15 cents would be sold within the temple courts for $15! This was shameless extortion, and abuse of the system is what caused such righteous anger in Jesus.

After learning the historical context, how do you feel about Jesus' actions now?

Have you ever experienced any type of injustice?

There is one additional reason Jesus causes this commotion. The place where the vendors and moneychangers are selling is in the Court of the Gentiles. During this time, Gentiles (non-Jewish persons) were not allowed to enter the temple to worship God. There was only one place designated where they could freely worship the Lord. Jesus is angered because the vendors and moneylenders have blocked the Gentiles from their place of worship and prayer.

From the very beginning, the mission of God has been to ransom a people for Himself from every tribe, tongue, language, and people. God formed the nation of Israel to serve as a light to

> *God welcomes home anyone who will have him and, in fact, has made the first move already."*
>
> PHILIP YANCEY,
> WHAT'S SO AMAZING ABOUT GRACE?

The Temple: *The holy place where man and God were reconciled, where sins were forgiven, and worship occured.*

the nations. When God created a covenant with Abraham (the father of the Israelites), He told him:

> *Go from your country and your kindred and your father's house to the land that I will show you. And I will make of you a great nation, and I will bless you and make your name great, so that you will be a blessing. I will bless those who bless you, and him who dishonors you I will curse, and in you all the families of the earth shall be blessed.*
> — Genesis 12:1–3

God said that He would make Abraham into a great nation. God also declared that He would bless the world through them. Why? Because Israel was God's chosen instrument to point the world to Himself. Through the nation of Israel, the Messiah, Jesus, would come into the world to save sinners who turned to Him in faith. Through Israel, God established His law, the priesthood, the Temple, the sacrificial system, and the annual feasts. All of these pointed to Jesus, the Messiah, who was to come.

The Temple was the place where the priests would offer sacrifices daily to God on behalf of sin. They would do this on the altar in the middle of the Temple, but Gentiles were only permitted to worship in the outer court. It was there that the moneychangers and merchants set up their business. By doing so, they had occupied the only place that a Gentile could worship the living God.

Thus, we see the righteous indignation of the Son of God. He turns over the tables of the moneychangers and drives the merchants out with a scourge of cords. The very nation that was to be a blessing to the world was not allowing the world to be blessed. As the Savior of the world, Jesus couldn't let that stand.

"I will make you as a light for the nations, that my salvation may reach to the end of the earth."

ISAIAH 49:6

Read Isaiah 49:6 in the margin. What does it tell you about the Messiah's mission?

Read Isaiah 56:7 in the margin. What was God's intended purpose for the Temple?

> "For my house shall be called a house of prayer for all peoples."
> ISAIAH 56:7B

Read John 2:18–24.

How did the Jewish leaders respond to the commotion Jesus caused (verse 18)?

Please note, the leaders do not ask Jesus "why are you cleansing?", but "what gives you the right?" They are aware of the corruption but wanted to know by whose authority Jesus did this act.

What "sign" does Jesus say will validate His right to cleanse the Temple (verse 19)?

When Jesus mentions "the Temple" being destroyed, what Temple does He mean (verse 21)?

How does it make you feel to know that Jesus knew before it happened that He would die and be resurrected?

The cleansing of the Temple was a sign. The purpose of a sign is to point to something greater. In this act, Jesus demonstrated the Father's heart for justice, integrity, and truth. This scene also reveals His heart for all nations to come to the Light.

> "The Temple was the greatest Jewish symbol, and Jesus was challenging it, and proposing that His mission is to be what the Temple stood for to the people. He would be the place of atonement, reconciliation, worship, and the place where God dwells among them."
>
> N.T. WRIGHT, THE CHALLENGE OF JESUS

Read the following passages about God's heart for all nations, peoples, and races: Psalm 22:27; Psalm 86:9; Isaiah 45:22

What do you discover about God's heart and mission in these verses?

After reviewing these passages, it is easy to understand Jesus' zeal for His Father's house. His righteous anger at the injustice and blocking of the Gentile court seems completely justified. Taking a whip and driving out those who stood in the way of worship and prayer reveals both Jesus' heart and mission.

John wants us to see Jesus for who He is, the one who offers all that the Temple symbolized—access to God's presence. When Christ cleansed the Temple, He declared that the old system was broken, and He came to inaugurate a new way—through His body. As we proceed through our study, Jesus' mission becomes more evident. But, for now, let His passion speak to your heart—Jesus cleared the way for you!

Take a minute to praise Jesus for His passion and for making a way for all peoples and nations to come to the Father. Use this space to express your worship and praise.

BEHOLD AND BELIEVE

Video Teaching Notes

Video teachings available for free at www.beholdandbelieve.com.

WEEK 2: BEHOLD, THE LAMB

The next day he saw Jesus coming toward him, and said, "Behold, the Lamb of God, who takes way the sin of the world." — John 1:29

I. Why does Jesus need to take away sin; Genesis 3:1–13

The moment they broke the skin of the fruit, all creation groaned. Lust, shame, fear, guilt, mistrust, blame-shifting, and loneliness rushed into their hearts. As if waking up from a blissful dream, they saw for the first time they were naked. It was humiliating, so they made coverings for themselves out of the fig leaves. For the first time in their lives, they questioned whether being exposed to each other—and to God—was safe. There they stood; uncovered, ashamed, and awakened to sin. — Russ Ramsey

Guilt says: _____

Shame says: _____

II. God pursues us and God covers our shame; Genesis 3:14–21

Redemption is **promised** is in the Garden of Eden. God made a promise to the Serpent that the _____ would one day come who would crush his head. (Genesis 3:15–16)

Redemption is **modeled** is in the Garden of Eden. God took an animal, sacrificed it, and used the skin of the animal to _____ the nakedness of Adam and Eve. This was the very first act of substitutionary atonement. (Genesis 3:21)

III. The Revelation of the Lamb of God
Background: The Abrahamic Covenant   Genesis 12:1–3

Genesis 22:1–14 — This story is key to understanding why Jesus is called the Lamb of God.

John 19:16–18

The soldiers took Jesus, carrying his own _____.
He went out of the place of the Skull (which in Aramaic is called Golgotha).

This is the _____ where the lamb died in the place of Isaac.

> For God so loved the world that He gave His one and only Son, that whoever believes in Him shall not perish but have eternal life. For God did not send His Son into the world to condemn the world, but to save the world through Him.
> — John 3:16–17

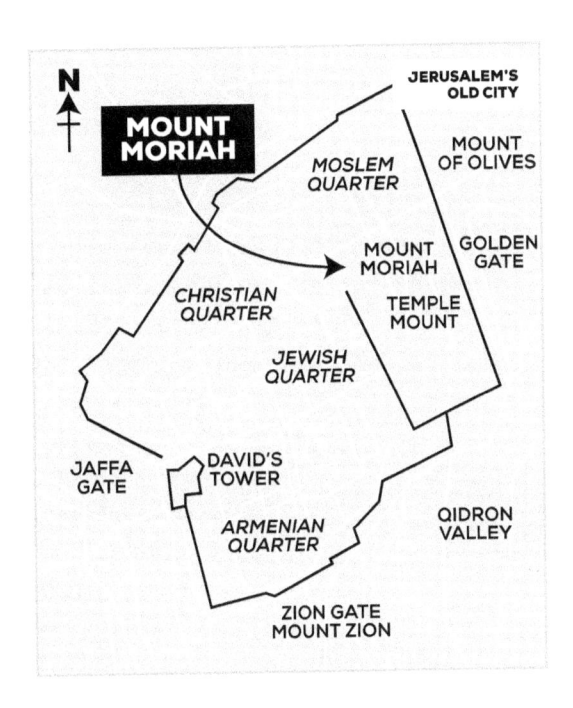

SMALL GROUP QUESTIONS

1. What did you behold about Jesus in your homework this week? What did this revelation lead you to believe?
2. Based on all you learned in today's teaching, why is Jesus rightly called the Lamb of God?
3. Marian discussed how guilt and shame were the result of sin entering the human heart. What is the difference between guilt and shame?
4. Marian described how we use "fig leaves" to cover our shame. Some examples are perfectionism, people pleasing, religion, lying, addictions (alcohol, food, shopping) relationship avoidance, anger, and busyness. Which one could you identify with the most and why?
5. Read Psalm 34:1–5. What happens when one looks to the Lord in faith? What are we free from?
6. Now read John 3:16–17. Why did God the Father send His Son into the word? How does Jesus remedy our the issues of both guilt and shame?

WEEK 2

Day 1: John 3:1-21

> "We must see Nicodemus as a representative of all men standing as sinners before God."
>
> — J.M. BOICE

What is on your spiritual résumé? By this question, I mean, what are the accomplishments or activities you think would help you earn God's acceptance? For example, before I came into a real relationship with Jesus Christ, I put my hope in a spiritual résumé that read something like this:

- I grew up going to Sunday School, Vacation Bible School, and Youth Group.
- I celebrated Christmas and Easter.
- I knew some Bible stories.
- I worked at a Christian summer camp in college.

But here's the problem: none of these accomplishments or activities were enough to make me right with God. As the old saying goes, "Sitting in a garage doesn't make you a car and sitting in a church building doesn't make you a child of God." Today, in our study of John, we learn about the emptiness of our spiritual résumés and how all people need the supernatural work of God called regeneration.

Read John 3:1–21 then answer the following:
With whom is Jesus' meeting (verse 1)?

When does his meeting with Jesus take place?

What is Nicodemus's initial opinion of Jesus (verse 2)?

Concerning Nicodemus, Warren Weirsbe writes:

> *"Nicodemus was a Pharisee, which meant he lived by the strictest possible religious rules. Not all Pharisees were hypocrites (as one may infer from Jesus' comments recorded in Matt. 23), and evidence indicates that Nicodemus was deeply sincere in his quest for truth. He came to Jesus by night, not because he was afraid of being seen, but most likely because he wanted to have a quiet uninterrupted conversation with the new Teacher "come from God." Nicodemus was representing the religious leaders. He was a man of high moral character, deep religious hunger, and yet profound spiritual blindness."*[7]

John tells us that Nicodemus is a member of the Jewish ruling council, also known as the Sanhedrin. This group becomes extremely important later in John's Gospel and so does Nicodemus.

Read the Word Study: "Sanhedrin" in the margin. Considering this is such an important and select group, what does this suggest about Nicodemus?

Biblical scholars debate what motivated Nicodemus to meet with Jesus. Very likely Nicodemus was curious about Jesus and chose to form his opinions about Him from firsthand conversation. Most Pharisees were intensely jealous of Jesus because He challenged their authority and threatened their position of power. But Nicodemus was different.

In describing Nicodemus, Tim Keller says, "So here's a man who has it all together. Not only that. He's a member of the Sanhedrin,

---

Sanhedrin:
Nicodemus was a member of the Jewish ruling council. Although the Romans controlled Israel politically, the Jews were given some authority over religious and minor civil disputes. The Jewish ruling council (Sanhedrin) was made up of 71 of Israel's religious leaders. They functioned like the Supreme Court in the United States, handling civil and religious issues. Nicodemus was a very prominent figure in Israel, in fact, Jesus called him "a teacher of Israel" [†]

---

† Barton, B. B. (1993). *John* (p. 51). Wheaton, IL: Tyndale House.

> "From an early age, we are taught to be proud, strong, and independent. None of those things are wrong, but when it comes to our Christian life, the paradigm has to shift. Jesus invites us to rest, to trust, to depend on him."
>
> LOUIE GIGLIO, GOLIATH MUST FALL

which means he was a man of tremendous wealth and power. He has biblical knowledge, religious understanding, intellectual depth, power, civic-minded, wise, open, and wealthy. Jesus specifically comes after him and says, "You, Nicodemus. You. The one who has it all together. You need to be born again."[8]

How would you describe Nicodemus' spiritual resume? Is it a good one according to the world's standards?

In a sense, Nicodemus represents the best of humanity. He is extremely moral, he is a leader, he is educated, and a man of great status. He brings a great résumé to the table. But this is precisely the point: although on a human level it seems Nicodemus has done all the right things and checked all the boxes, this human effort is not what is required to enter the Kingdom of God and become His child.

According to verse 3–8, what does Jesus tell him is required to enter the Kingdom of God?

What is Nicodemus's reaction?

Jesus is clear with Nicodemus that He is not referring to a physical birth, but a spiritual one. In verse 8, Jesus says those who are "born again" are born of the Holy Spirit and this new birth occurs when one believes on Jesus for salvation. The human condition is so desperate that we all require a supernatural work of God. Our spiritual résumés are of no value. We need God to make us new creations, and this is the work of the Holy Spirit when we look to Jesus as our Savior.

The phrase "born again" literally means "born from above." Nicodemus had a real need. He needed a change of his heart—a spiritual transformation. New birth, being born again, is an act of God whereby eternal life is imparted to the person who believes.

Regeneration is another term that describes this new birth. Regeneration is the sovereign work of the Holy Spirit in granting spiritual life to each Christian.

Review the following passages about regeneration and share what you learn about the new birth: Ezekiel 36:26–27 and 2 Corintians 5:17 (In the margin).

What question does Nicodemus ask in John 3:9?

Here's the question most of us are probably asking at this point: How do I know if I am born again? Jesus says that the new birth is an act of the Holy Spirit, whom He compares to wind. We can't see wind: it is invisible. Still, we can see the evidence of it: balloons floating in the air, a flag whipping in the sky, or leaves blowing across a lawn—each is evidence of the wind moving.

The same is true of us. While we can't see the Holy Spirit, we can see proof if one is born of the Spirit.

- We have new desires to please God.
- We have new power to resist sin.
- We now exhibit Christ-like nature: love, joy, peace, and patience (to name a few).

We call this evidence the fruit of the Spirit. Just as an apple tree produces apples, a person born again will evidence the new life of Christ.

> *And I will give you a new heart, and a new spirit I will put within you. And I will remove the heart of stone from your flesh and give you a heart of flesh. And I will put my Spirit within you, and cause you to walk in my statutes and be careful to obey my rules.*
> EZEKIEL 36:26-27

> *If anyone is in Christ, he is a new creation. The old has passed away; behold, the new has come.*
> 2 CORINTHIANS 5:17

> As Moses lifted up the serpent in the wilderness, so must the Son of Man be lifted up, that whoever believes in him may have eternal life.
>
> JOHN 3:14-15

Jesus doesn't sugarcoat the truth with Nicodemus: our spiritual résumés are pointless. We require a supernatural work of God that makes us new. This new birth occurs when we lift our eyes and in faith behold Jesus.

Review John 3:14–15 in the margin and then read Numbers 21:4–9 for the backstory.

When Moses lifted the serpent up in the wilderness, the people were saved from their sin and death by looking to it. What does Jesus imply about Himself and His purpose by using this illustration?

Warren Weirsbe explains this statement:

> *Much as the serpent was lifted up on that pole, so the Son of God would be lifted up on a cross. Why? To save us from sin and death. In the camp of Israel, the solution to the "serpent problem" was not in killing the serpents, making medicine, pretending they were not there, passing anti-serpent laws, or climbing the pole. The answer was in looking by faith at the uplifted serpent.*
>
> *The whole world has been bitten by sin, and "the wages of sin is death" (Rom. 6:23). God sent His Son to die, not only for Israel, but for a whole world. How is a person born from above? How is he or she saved from eternal perishing? By believing on Jesus Christ; by looking to Him in faith.*[9]

What did a snake-bitten person have to believe in order to be saved from death?

Likewise, what must we believe in order to be saved from sin?

Write John 3:16.

Considering the context and the conversation between Jesus and this powerful man, how do you think Nicodemus would have felt about these words?

What do you learn about God the Father from John 3:16?

Why was Jesus sent into the world (verse 17)?

How does it make you feel about Jesus that He did not condemn you, but rather came to save you?

Charles Wesley spearheaded a movement with his brother John that would come to be called the Great Awakening. Together they also founded the Methodist Church. But all these things happened after Charles's own "great awakening."

Ironically, Wesley was much like Nicodemus. Wesley was religious. He was a pastor. He read and taught the Bible. Despite all of this, something was missing in his heart. He knew all about Jesus but did not have a personal experience of Jesus in his life. When Wesley was thirty-five years old, on May 24, 1738, he was in Aldersgate, London, and heard a reading of Romans. It was at that moment that he "felt his heart strangely warm," and in a flash, realized that God had given him His Holy Spirit.

Wesley goes down in history as one of the most prolific hymn writers of all time. He wrote the famous hymn, *"And Can It Be"* in celebration of the day he was born again.

> *Long my imprisoned spirit lay,*
> *Fast bound in sin and nature's night*
> *Thine eye diffused a quickening ray*
> *I woke, the dungeon flamed with light*
> *My chains fell off, my heart was free*
> *I rose, went forth, and followed Thee*
> *Amazing love! How can it be*
> *That Thou, my God shouldst die for me?*
> *—"And Can It Be," Charles Wesley*

Take a minute to marvel at the Father's love that moved Him to give His only Son for you. Use this space to express your adoration and thanksgiving.

Day 2: John 3:22-36

A "turf war" is an unfriendly dispute between rival groups over territory or a particular sphere of influence. These disputes can be mild, or they can become malicious. From kids fighting on the playground over the swing set, to rival gangs battling it out over territory rights on our cities' streets, these wars are ugly and often, deadly.

In today's text, we see a type of turf war. The text opens by telling us that Jesus and His disciples have traveled to the Judean countryside where John the Baptist, the man we met in our study last week, has been doing ministry for a while. The crowds followed

WEEK 2

John to this area to hear him speak and experience baptism. But now Jesus has moved into the area and the winds of change begin to blow.

Read John 3:22–36.

Who is with Jesus in this scene (verse 22)?

Before we dive further into this text, a little Jewish cultural background will be helpful. In the Bible, many people referred to Jesus as "Rabbi." In John 1:38, we learn that "Rabbi" means "Teacher." It was a term of honor bestowed on those who knew and taught the Scriptures. Jesus' ministry centered on making disciples that He later sent out to be the proclaimers of His Gospel.

Theologian David Dockery makes this incredible observation concerning Jesus' intentionality to make disciples:

> When students of the life of Christ list the priorities of His ministry, many items come to mind: the miracles, the crucifixion, and of course, the resurrection. But one of the most significant items on Jesus' agenda is found in this: "Jesus and His disciples went out into the Judean countryside, where He spent some time with them." Jesus took twelve men and poured His life into theirs, discipling them in thought and deed in order that they might become the foundation of the church following His death, burial, and resurrection.[10]

The context of John 3:22–36 is discipleship. For several years, John the Baptist has seen his ministry grow and reach thousands throughout Israel. Now Jesus comes on the scene and the masses begin to flock to Him, even many of John's own disciples. In our day and age, this would cause bitter jealousy, name calling, frustration, and a whole host of marketing schemes to win back the followers. But this is not how John the Baptist reacted to this situation.

Rabbi:
Jewish rabbis would take on disciples who followed them, lived with them, and received training from them in specific interpretations of Jewish law. Each rabbi had his own opinion, and their teaching was referred to as a "yoke." This list of regulations ruling one's behavior is what Jesus referred to when He said, "My yoke is easy, and my burden is light" (Matthew 11:30). He meant that His teaching would not add to God's law placing undue burdens on His followers the way so many other rabbis' "yokes" were prone to do.

> "We can either choose to cling to starring roles in the little-bitty stories of us or opt to exchange our fleeting moment in the spotlight for a supporting role in the eternally beautiful epic that is the Story of God."
>
> LOUIE GIGLIO,
> I AM NOT BUT
> I KNOW I AM

Let's dig into text and discover how John the Baptist reacts to Jesus' popularity:

What do John's disciples report to him in verse 26?

In your own words, summarize John's attitude and reaction in verses 28–30.

Does John engage in a turf war with Jesus?

Keep in mind that in John 1:19–33, John the Baptist gave powerful witness to Jesus' identity. When questioned by the religious authorities whether John was the Messiah, he boldly denied it and instead pointed them to Jesus. He identified Jesus as the Lamb of God who takes away the sin of the world. So now, when John sees Jesus stepping into His destiny, he is not filled with jealousy; he is filled with joy.

John the Baptist uses a beautiful example to illustrate why he is filled with joy. The illustration he uses is of a Bride, her Groom, and the "friend of the bridegroom." John casts himself in a wedding scene. In Jewish culture, the best man or the "friend of the bridegroom" played an important role. He was the one to announce that the groom was coming to take away his bride to the marriage feast.

With great humility, John essentially says, "It's not about me. My role is to get the bride ready and let her know the groom is here, then I step back and watch the wedding take place." Warren Wiersbe notes, "What a foolish thing it would be for the best man to try to 'upstage' the Bridegroom and take his place. John's joy was to hear the voice of the Bridegroom and know that He had claimed His bride."

In the space below, write John the Baptist's famous words from verse 30.

Now we discover why John is so adamant with his disciples that Jesus must increase. John recognizes that Jesus is not just another rabbi; He is heaven sent, He is the hope of humanity, He is God in the flesh.

Read John 3:31–35.

Whose words does Jesus speak (verse 34)?

One scholar explains, "The one who accepts Jesus and the truth of His message avoids God's wrath, participates in the life of the Spirit, and has life eternal. That life is not as a gift in the future but life eternal as a present reality that begins at the moment Jesus is accepted in faith and engaged in relationship."[11]

I find it interesting that John loves his disciples enough to do two things uncommon in our culture today. First, he encourages them to follow Jesus instead of him. He wants Jesus' ministry to increase and his own to decrease. Second, John was not afraid to speak hard truth. He understands that Jesus was the Lamb of God and His sacrifice would take the wrath of God against sin for those who put their hope in Christ. But John pulls no punches by saying, Jesus is your only hope … trust in Him … there is no other way to be saved. There is no plan B. Jesus is the only way!

Ouch! That kind of talk does not fly in our world of cancel culture. Yet John's love for his disciples eclipses his fear of man. He is more concerned about their eternity than he is about his own popularity. Apart from Jesus' sacrificial death, there is no payment for our sin, and we are still under wrath instead of grace. It takes a great deal of love to be so truthful.

What do we learn about God the Father in verse 35?

What is true of those who believe in Jesus, according to verse 36?

Friends, the ultimate turf war is the one that happens every single day—it is the war for our hearts. John the Baptist reveals the heart of a man who is entirely devoted to the glory of God. He willingly laid down his fame and popularity so that Jesus would be lifted high. He understood that promoting Jesus was his ultimate mission. John's ministry paved the way for Jesus to step into human history and fulfill His divine purpose as the Savior of the world!

Take a minute to consider: What is your role in the story of God's glory? How does Jesus want to use your life to shine a spotlight on Him? Use this space to talk to God, and if you are ready, to surrender everything to Him to be used for His glory.

Day 3: John 4:1-44

In our study this week, we've met Nicodemus, a good man whose spiritual résumé was not enough to qualify him for the kingdom of God. Nicodemus displayed the best credentials, but these could not remedy the problem of sin. Today we meet a woman who is his opposite. By the world's standards, she has nothing in which to boast. Both have a God-size problem that requires God-size grace.

One scholar observes the striking contrast on display in these two encounters with Jesus:

> *It is difficult to imagine a greater contrast between two persons than the contrast between the important and sophisticated Nicodemus, this ruler of the Jews, and the simple Samaritan woman. He was a Jew; she a Samaritan. He was a Pharisee; she belonged to no religious party. He was a politician; she had no status whatever. He was a scholar; she was uneducated. He was highly moral; she was immoral. He had a name; she is nameless. He was a man; she was a woman. He came at night, to protect his reputation; she, who had no reputation, came at noon. Nicodemus came seeking; the woman was sought by Jesus.*[12]

Both Nicodemus and the woman we meet today have a longing in their souls that nothing in this material world can satisfy. Nicodemus attempts to fill his emptiness through religion and education, and while respectable, neither are successful at satisfying the human heart. The second, a nameless woman with a bad reputation, attempts to fill her longings with romantic love and sexual encounters. While her path carries more shame, it proves just as empty.

What is this longing that they both hold in common? Both have hearts that are wired for and in desperate need of a relationship with God. They give evidence to the fact that nothing in this world will satisfy the ache of the soul other than God Himself. As Saint Augustine confesses:

> *Thou hast made us for Thyself, and our hearts are restless until they find their rest in Thee.*[13]

Read John 4:1–6.

Where is Jesus going (verse 3)?

The Sixth Hour: *On the Hebrew clock, the hours were counted from sunrise to sunset (roughly 6 a.m. to 6 p.m.), so the "sixth hour" was around noon.* † *The time of day, hence intensity of heat, also would probably cue the audience that this was not the time when most of the women would come to draw— hence lead the reader to consider why this woman came to the well alone.*‡

---

† Barry, J. D., Mangum, D., Brown, D. R., Heiser, M. S., Custis, M., Ritzema, E., … Bomar, D. (2012, 2016). *Faithlife Study Bible* (Jn 4:6). Bellingham, WA: Lexham Press.

‡ Keener, C. S. (2012). *The Gospel of John: A Commentary* (Vol. 1, p. 593). Grand Rapids, MI: Baker Academic.

What time is it (verse 6)?

Before plunging into this conversation, a little historical context will help us understand its radical nature. First, in Jesus' day, the Jewish people generally hated Samaritans. These racial tensions went back for centuries, and it was common practice for Jews to sidestep the region of Samaria to avoid meeting the people. We should also note how most men viewed women in that day. Females were highly discriminated against, and a righteous rabbi would not deem to look at or even speak to a woman. Thus, as we see Jesus with this unnamed woman, we see that He was counter-cultural and was not held captive to man's prejudices or pride.

Jesus turned the tables to include women in ministry and treated them with respect. We can't take for granted the significance of the small gesture of a conversation. How Jesus treats the woman at the well with dignity sets a precedent to His followers of how all women should be treated.

Read John 4:7–15.

What does Jesus ask of this woman (verse 7)?

How does she respond to His request? What is her attitude (verse 9)?

What does Jesus offer her (verse 10)?

What promise does Jesus make concerning the water He gives (verse 14)?

The woman has no clue that this Jewish Rabbi is the Creator of the World and the One for whom her soul was formed. Yet, despite her obliviousness, Jesus engages her in a conversation by asking her for a drink. The fact that Jesus even speaks to her is startling. After all, she comes to the well at noon, a time when most people are at home taking afternoon siesta. We will soon discover that she's a social outcast in her community, which explains why she visits the well when it's sweltering instead of early in the cooler hours of the day (see Word Study: The Sixth Hour).

So, beyond the differences that existed between a Jewish rabbi and a Samaritan woman, she also carries a huge bucket of shame to that well. She was most likely accustomed to being ignored or mistreated by those she encountered there.

Read John 4:15. What does the woman ask of Jesus?

Jesus used physical truths to illustrate spiritual realities. This woman is living with a spiritual thirst. Jesus uses her need for physical water to expose her soul's desperate need for God.

In the Bible, water is a consistent symbol for God. Without access to this life-giving substance, the human body will shut down within three days. Just as our bodies need water to live, so our souls require a relationship with God. One of my favorite quotes by Blaise Pascal says it best:

> There is a God-shaped vacuum in the heart of each man which cannot be satisfied by any created thing but only by God the Creator, made known through Jesus Christ.

Living Water:

In Jewish speech the phrase "living water" meant water that was flowing, like water in a river or stream, as opposed to water that was stagnant, as in a well. Living water was considered to be better. Therefore, she wanted to know where Jesus had found such water. From the tone of her remarks it is evident that she even thought his claim a bit blasphemous, for it was a claim to have done something greater than her ancestor Jacob had been able to do. [†]

[†] Boice, J. M. (2005). *The Gospel of John: an Expositional Commentary* (p. 279). Grand Rapids, MI: Baker Books.

Sin is our attempt to fill the "God-shaped vacuum" with something other than God. This attempt can take many forms. In this woman's case, as we will see, she used romantic relationships and sex to fill the God-shaped hole, but her attempt was in vain. Because no man, no matter how wonderful, charming, or handsome, can do for us what only God was designed to do—quench the thirst of our souls.

I know this one from experience. If there is any Biblical character that I can relate to, it is the woman at the well. I know first-hand what it feels like to try to find love and to fill my emptiness with the fleeting pleasures of this world. I lived that life for many years until Jesus rescued me from myself! That's exactly what He does for this woman—He rescues her from the emptiness of her existence by exposing her desperate thirst. Her condition is the same as ours, sin is an attempt to meet a legitimate need in an illegitimate way.

What are some ways you've been recently tempted to quench your thirst for God in an "illegitimate" way?

Now that the woman is eager for living water, Jesus turns her attention to her sin, not to shame her, but to expose her soul's thirst and point her to the One who can quench it.

Read John 4:16–24.

How do you think the woman feels when Jesus asks her to go call her husband?

What does Jesus reveal that He knows about her?

What title does she give to Jesus in verse 19?

Jesus saw into her heart. I believe He saw the dashed hopes and dreams of not one, but five failed marriages. I believe He saw the shame she carried because she was now living a life of adultery. I believe He saw the hurt she carried after being excluded from society because of her lifestyle. Jesus saw past the tough exterior and saw a broken woman who needed healing, hope, and forgiveness. Offering water to a thirsty soul, He extended her the cup of grace.

Read John 4:20–23 and note what she does after deciding Jesus is a prophet.

Like many of us when our sin is exposed, we try to change the subject or deflect from the awkwardness of being honest. This woman does both. She attempts to raise a religious debate about the proper place of worship so to distract Jesus from seeing the real issue—her soul's thirst.

Read John 4:25–26 and see how this dramatic conversation ends. What incredible revelation does Jesus make in verse 26?

While this is astonishing, unfortunately, the full weight of Jesus' reply doesn't register in English. His words seem to express no more than the claim: "I am the Messiah." To be precise, His words are a title. Jesus does not really say, "I am he." The "he" was added by English translators. He simply said, "I am."

The title "I am" was the great Old Testament name for God: Jehovah, the title He proclaimed to Moses at the burning bush. In this moment, Jesus affirms His identity as the Messiah (whom both the Jews and Samaritans were expecting) and goes a step further by revealing to this woman that He is God: the life-giving, soul-quenching, grace-offering Lord Most High.

Oh, what a Savior! Jesus' love is not limited to the elite or polished. He intentionally went out of His way to reveal His identity to someone who desperately needed to know that she had not sinned beyond the reach of the mercy of God. His intentional pursuit speaks volumes and reveals more than just a title; it shows us His heart. Now let's conclude our study by looking at how Jesus transformed this woman's life and how she was used by God.

Read John 4:27–33.

What was the woman's testimony when she returned to her village (verse 29)?

What was the result of her testimony (verses 39–42)?

We began today by contrasting Nicodemus and this unnamed woman. The point of these stories is that both the religious man and the notorious woman needs grace and are welcome to it. If Nicodemus is an example that no one can rise so high as to be above salvation, the woman is an example of the fact that none of us can sink too low. It is not an accident that John placed these two beautiful stories together at the beginning of his Gospel. He wants us to know that God's grace is available for everyone, no matter their status, and today this grace is available for you.

Take a minute to marvel that Jesus revealed His identity to a woman whom the world considered an outcast. Use this space to express your adoration and thanksgiving.

Day 4: John 4:45–5:47

My daughter's terrorized screams woke me from a sound sleep around 2 a.m. Even in the middle of the night, a momma can discern if a situation is critical. Her cry was not the normal hungry wail of a newborn, or the whine of a wet diaper, or the frustrated pout of a toddler. The sound coming from Sydney's nursery was one that I'd never heard: it was terror—and it sent me bolting to her bedroom.

Lifting Sydney from her bed, I felt fever radiating from her body. The scariest part was not the blazing heat but the hysteria of her mind. She clawed at her skin. She screamed uncontrollably, and between frightened sobs we pieced together that she thought snakes and rats were crawling on her. My baby's temperature was so high that she was hallucinating.

Friends, that was the scariest night of my life. I'm forever thankful for a husband who remains calm in a crisis. Calm is not the word I would use to describe myself at that moment. I hit the floor, praying for God to do something as Justin set in motion an emergency room visit. We drove a few miles to the nearest ER and rushed our baby into the brightly lit waiting room.

A few hours later, the doctor and nurses got Sydney's fever down and this momma's heartbeat returned to a normal rhythm. While this emergency was thankfully short-lived, it impressed upon me the sheer desperation a parent feels when her child is in danger. "Desperate" is the exact word I would use to describe myself that night—I would have given any amount of money, I would have given all of my blood, I would have driven anywhere at any time—for someone to help my baby.

I share this story because we begin a section of John's Gospel that reveals the healing power of Christ. When Jesus stepped into our broken world, He was confronted by the full extent of human suffering. The blind, lame, sick, and broken heard of Jesus' power and brought their desperation to Him. As news of Jesus' power spread from village to village, the masses swarmed Him, and brought their suffering to the feet of the Great Physician.

Behold, I am the Lord, the God of all flesh. Is there anything too hard for me?
JEREMIAH 32:27

Today we look at two different healings performed by Jesus and the harsh reaction of the religious authorities. The first miracle comes at the request of a frantic father who begs for the life of his child. The second one occurs because Jesus sought out the recipient and extends to him God's mercy—the beneficiary was blessed without doing one single thing to earn the blessing.

Read John 4:46–54 and behold the power of Christ.

What is the location (verse 1)? What miracle did Jesus previously perform in this city?

Who is the desperate person in this story?

What does the text tell us about this father?

John tells us that the father is a nobleman. Scholars believe he was most likely a royal official in the court of King Herod. This means the "nobleman" is a man of great means and political power. We will discover that Jesus is not influenced by wealth or fame, but He is motivated by faith. He does not perform this miracle because the man is a Roman dignitary, but rather because of the need of the child and the faith of the father.

It's easy to imagine that the nobleman heard of the miracle Jesus performed in Cana, turning the water to wine. Therefore, when he found himself in a situation that his wealth, status, and privilege couldn't fix, he turned in desperation to a man who was rumored to work miracles.

Think back to a moment when you felt desperate for help. What was the situation and where did you turn?

WEEK 2

Look carefully at the text. How did Jesus heal the child?

In verse 50, we see Jesus speak the words, "Your son will live," and then we see the nobleman's response. What was his reaction?

What do you think yours would have been in that situation?

In your own words, how did Jesus perform this miracle?

> "There is no cancer, no sickness, no sin, no reversal of fortunes, no curse, no heartache—nothing that's greater than Jesus. Jesus heals. Jesus restores. Jesus brings life."
>
> LOUIE GIGLIO,
> THE COMEBACK

The details given in these verses inform us that the healing occurred at the precise moment Jesus spoke the words, "Your son lives!" Jesus' miracles were not mere illusions, tricks, or fantasy. Although the nobleman's son was roughly twenty miles away, he was healed at the exact time Jesus spoke the word. Here's the point: distance was no problem. Jesus Christ has mastery over space and time. This miracle was so evident to the nobleman and his servants that it produced faith throughout the entire household.[14]

What does this miracle reveal to you about Jesus?

Now the scene shifts. This time, we don't see a desperate family member racing to find Jesus, nor do we see the sufferer pressing through crowds to reach Him. We observe Jesus intentionally going to a man who is helpless, and it seems has given up hope. This man is a recipient of a miracle that he didn't even ask for but desperately needed.

Read John 5:1–9.

Where does this miracle take place?

What reason does the paralyzed man give for being at the pool for 38 years?

What does Jesus ask him?

Why do you think Jesus asked him this question?

What command does Jesus give (verse 8)?

This miracle demonstrates God's grace and mercy. This man is in a pitiable condition. He has been afflicted for thirty-eight years and lacks the power to change his situation. But see the grace of God at work in this man's story. Even though the man doesn't know Jesus or expect a miracle, God extends mercy to him. It should be noted that "Bethesda" means "house of grace," and this is what it became for this one man.

What does "grace" mean? Warren Weirsbe writes, "It means kindness to those who are undeserving. Jesus saw a multitude of sick people—but He chose only one man and healed him! This man was no more deserving than the others, but God chose him. This is a beautiful picture of salvation, and how it ought to humble us to know that we are chosen, in Him, and not because of our own merits but because of His grace (Ephesians 1:4)."[15]

Read John 5:10–18.

Why does the healing upset the Jews, or religious leaders (Verses 10, 16–18)?

One scholar observes, "This miracle should have revealed to the Jews in Jerusalem that the Messiah was finally present, for Isaiah had prophesied, then will the eyes of the blind be opened and the ears of the deaf unstopped. Then will the lame leap like a deer, and the mute tongue shout for joy, (Isaiah 35:5–6). Instead, they chose to focus on another issue: The day on which this took place was a Sabbath."[16]

In the New Testament, Jesus and His disciples observed the Sabbath—but Jesus declared it to be a day created by God for man's good, not man's oppression. He healed on the Sabbath and even declared Himself Lord over the Sabbath (Mark 2:23–28). Jesus' failure to comply with their many rules and restrictions brought heated conflict.[17]

What two reasons did they give for wanting to kill Jesus (verse 18)?

Here we are introduced to a theme that proves vital to the rest of this Gospel. Jesus performs miracles, or what John calls "signs." Instead of faith, as one would expect, many respond with vigorous resistance. You've probably heard the expression, "Don't miss the forest for the trees." This aptly describes what occurred in John 5. The religious leaders were more concerned with the man carrying his mat on the Sabbath than with his miraculous healing.[18]

So, when Jesus is confronted with the fact that He healed a man on the Sabbath, He doesn't defend His actions by educating the leaders on their mistaken beliefs. Instead, Jesus essentially says, "I'm doing the work of my Father." And it is this response—the claim that God is His Father—that is the ultimate reason they plot together to destroy him.

Sabbath:
From the time of creation, the seventh day was a special day set aside by God for rest. The Hebrew word shabbat, "Sabbath," means "to cease," "to desist," or "to rest." In the Old Testament, while ordinary work ceased on this day, sacred activities were encouraged. The weekly Sabbath was a great gift to God's people, but as time went on, the leaders added more and more restrictions to the Sabbath, that detoured from God's original intention for the day. †

---

† Bruce, B. J. (2003). Sabbath. In C. Brand, C. Draper, A. England, S. Bond, E. R. Clendenen, & T. C. Butler (Eds.), *Holman Illustrated Bible Dictionary* (p. 1426). Nashville, TN: Holman Bible Publishers.

> But the testimony that I have is greater than that of John. For the works that the Father has given me to accomplish, the very works that I am doing, bear witness about me that the Father has sent me.
>
> JOHN 5:36

Read John 5:19–47.

List a few things Jesus reveals to us about God the Father in verses 19–23.

Name a few things Jesus claims about His own identity.

What connection does Jesus make between belief and eternal life (verses 24–25)?

What does Jesus say His signs (miracles) testify to? (Read verse 36 in the margin.)

In His defense, Jesus publicly identifies Himself with God the Father and goes on at length to prove His claim is valid. This claim is validated not only by Jesus' miracles, but by the Scriptures themselves. He essentially says that any who reject Him stand accused by the very book they claim to believe, because it all points to Him.

What we see from this interaction and Jesus' response to His accusers is that there is always a response to Jesus. Some fall down in worship. Some walk away in disgust. But one cannot remain neutral when faced with the question of His identity.

As C. S. Lewis famously said:

> A man who was merely a man and said the sort of things Jesus said would not be a great moral teacher. He would either be a lunatic—on a level with the man who says he is a poached egg—or

else He would be the Devil of Hell. You must make your choice. Either this man was, and is, the Son of God, or else a madman or something worse. You can shut Him up for a fool, you can spit at Him and kill Him as a demon, or you can fall at His feet and call Him Lord and God. But let us not come with any patronizing nonsense about His being a great human teacher. He has not left that open to us. He did not intend to.[19]

Friend, we all must make a choice—what will I do with Jesus? His miracles prove and His teachings testify that He is the Son of God. And yet, we must all choose for ourselves. Will we behold His glory and choose to believe? Or, like many who were eyewitnesses to the miracles, will we walk away in unbelief?

Today we've seen so many different responses to Jesus. The nobleman responded to the miracle of his son's healing with faith, and so did his entire household. But, on the other hand, the religious leaders responded to Jesus healing the lame man with hardened hearts and plotted to kill Him.

As you ponder your personal response, consider this: each of us is symbolized by the man at the pool of Bethesda. We desperately need God's mercy, and His miracle beautifully illustrates the Gospel. God comes to us and offers us a new life, brought by the miracle called grace, where by His power, we are healed, forgiven, and made whole. But first, Jesus asks us, "Do you want to be healed?"

Take a minute to marvel at Jesus' power to perform miracles. Bring your burden, desperation, and need for fresh grace to the One who is the Great Physician.

Video Teaching Notes

Video teachings available for free at www.beholdandbelieve.com.

WEEK 3: BEHOLD, THE GREAT I AM

Jesus answered, "I tell you the truth, before Abraham was even born, I Am!"
— John 8:58

I. John's Purpose in Writing the Gospel; John 20:31

What comes into our minds when we think about God is the most important thing about us. — A. W. Tozer

II. The Revelation of the Great I AM; Exodus 3:1–15

I Am or Yahweh is God's covenant name, which is translated as LORD over 6,800 times in the Old Testament. This name reveals that He is the self-existent, eternal, creator, who has no equal or rival. This is the holy, covenant name of God.

III. The Audacity of Jesus; John 8:58–59

It was our Lord's claim to equality with the Father that outraged the religionist of His day and led at last to His crucifixion. — A. W. Tozer

I am trying here to prevent anyone from saying the really foolish thing that people often say about Him: I'm ready to accept Jesus as a great moral teacher, but I don't accept his claim to be God. That is the only thing we must not say. A man who was merely a man and said the sort of things that Jesus said would not be a great moral teacher. He would either be a lunatic ... or else he would be the Devil of Hell. You must make a choice. Either this man was, and is the Son of God, or else a madman or something worse. You can shut him up for a fool, you can spit at him and kill him as a demon or you can fall at his feet and call him Lord and God, but let us not come with any patronizing nonsense about his being a great human teacher. He has not left that open to us. — C. S. Lewis

IV. The 7 "I AM" Statements of Jesus in the Gospel of John

I AM _____ John 6:35, 41
I AM _____ John 8:12
I AM _____ John 10:7–9
I AM _____ John 11:25
I AM _____ John 10:11
I AM _____ John 14:6
I AM _____ John 15:1–5

The special revelation which this name gives is that of the grace of God. 'I Am' is an unfinished sentence. It has no object. I Am—what? Great is our wonder when we discover, as we continue on with our Bibles, that He is saying, 'I Am whatever my people need,' and that the sentence is purposely left blank so that man may bring his many and various needs, as they arise, to Him to complete it. — Roy Hession, We Would See Jesus

V. When God Speaks His Name; John 18:1–8

SMALL GROUP QUESTIONS

1. What did you behold about Jesus in your homework this week? What did this revelation lead you to believe?

2. What was John's stated purpose in writing this Gospel? John 20:31

3. Read and discuss the C. S. Lewis quote found in today's video lecture notes (page 62). Why is Jesus not merely a "good teacher?"

4. What makes Jesus claim found in John 8:58–59 so audacious or outrageous?

5. Which of the Jesus' "I Am" statements is the most meaningful to you at this point in your faith journey? Why?

6. Read Philippians 2:9–11. How was this truth portrayed when Jesus spoke "I Am" in the Garden of Gethsemane? What does this tell us about Jesus' power and person?

WEEK 3

Day 1: John 6:1-21

"The more, the merrier" has always been my motto. I love hosting people in my home. Even if a dinner party was originally planned for 6 people, I'll easily added 10 more folks to the fun before the big day arrives. I can't help myself. I'll see someone at church or run into someone at the grocery store, and before you know it, I've invited them, their dog, and their cousins and asked them to bring some pie.

But here's the problem, the moment always comes—about 15 minutes before the guests walk through the door—when I begin to fret. I start pacing the kitchen and pestering my husband with this question: Do you think we have enough food?

Granted, we always have enough food. I usually have leftovers coming out of my ears. My fear of shortage is rooted in the fact that I'm from a huge family—7 kids, to be exact. Having plenty of food was an art form that my mother mastered, and I'm still unsure how she did it.

Therefore, when I read today's scripture, I feel a knot tighten in my stomach. As I imagine the myriad of hungry people sitting at the feet of Jesus, the hostess in me gets a little frantic at the impossible task before the disciples to feed all of them!

Here's a fact: Impossible situations are God's specialty. This is the point John drives home in the two stories we read today. The miraculous is not difficult for Jesus. After all, as the Creator of the World, He made all things from nothing, so how hard could it be for Him to multiply food to feed hungry people? And as the Maker of Heaven and Earth, how hard is it for Jesus to walk on the very water that He spoke into existence?

Read John 6:1–15.

Describe in your own words the scene and this miracle.

This is the only miracle recorded in all four Gospels. One can only imagine that it made quite an impression on each of the disciples. So much so that whenever they testified about Jesus, they were sure to share this story. For that reason, let's look at this miracle from the vantage point of another disciple who witnessed it.

Take a minute to read this miracle in Mark 6:31–44 and note what you learn about the context.

According to Mark 6:31, what is Jesus' intention when He takes the disciples to a deserted place?

Mark 6:34 tells us that Jesus is moved with compassion when He sees the crowds. But the disciples are tired and want some rest. What recommendation do the disciples give to Jesus in Mark 6:36?

Clearly, the disciples were exhausted. I get it. As someone who has been in ministry for 20-plus years, I know the toll can be tough. But the point of this story is to show us the inadequacy of human strength and our desperate need for heavenly supply. Therefore, Jesus doesn't send them away, He provides for their need.

Denarius:
"A denarius, which was worth approximately seventeen cents, was a day's wage for an unskilled laborer. If a man worked for six days a week, two hundred denarii would represent the pay for thirty-three weeks, which would be just about eight months. It would take a long time to save the equivalent of such a sum. No doubt none of the disciples would have enough money to subsidize the purchase of food for a crowd of approximately ten thousand persons, including women and children." †

---

† Tenney, M. C. (1981). John. In F. E. Gaebelein (Ed.), *The Expositor's Bible Commentary: John and Acts* (Vol. 9, p. 71). Grand Rapids, MI: Zondervan Publishing House.

Read John 6:5–7.

Which disciple does Jesus ask where to get food for the masses?

What is his response?

Philip is the natural person to ask where food might be found, for his home is nearby, Bethsaida. But John clarifies that the question is a test for Philip rather than a request for the closest burger joint. Jesus is asking the question to see if Philip believes in His ability to provide.

Bless Philip's heart, he does a little mental arithmetic, and his calculations tell him that the need is beyond his own pay grade. Philip's reply stresses the hopelessness of the situation—two hundred denarii's worth of bread would not be enough. As Leon Morris notes, "Philip does not point to a solution, but to an impossibility."[20]

According to John 6:8–9, what is brought to Jesus? Does this seem enough to solve the problem at hand?

Read John 6:10–13.

What does Jesus do first (verses 10–11)?

Using your imagination, how do you think John and the other disciples feel as they watch in astonishment while the food multiplies?

WEEK 3

How much food is left over after everyone was full?

John 6:14–15 tells us the crowd's response to this miracle.

What does Jesus do instead (verse 15)?

The multitude's desire to crown Jesus as king indicates both the growth of His popularity and a moment of decision for Him. The masses wanted someone to rule them who would feed them and defeat their Roman oppressors; they did not understand His true mission. Jesus, on the other hand, refused to become a political pawn. He did not come to establish an earthly kingdom at this time. His calling was far greater and required sacrifice, and He would not be deterred from His heavenly assignment.

The miracle is one more sign that proves Jesus' identity as the long-awaited Messiah. If this miracle stood alone, we would have ample reason to worship Jesus, but it does not. Instead, it is presented with another clear sign that Jesus is more than just a good teacher. He is more than just a prophet. He is God in the flesh.

Read John 6:16–21.
What do you love about this story?

What does Jesus say to the disciples when they see Him on the water (verse 20)?

> "Enemy-occupied territory—that is what this world is. Christianity is the story of how the rightful king is calling us to take part in a great campaign of sabotage."
> C.S. LEWIS,
> MERE CHRISTIANITY

Do you ever struggle with fear? Do you ever battle worry or anxiety? To overcome fear, anxiety, and worry, we must fix our gaze on something or someone we believe can change the situation. Over the years, I've learned that faith drives out fear. Biblical faith isn't just wishful thinking, it is a confident expectation of good that is rooted in the character and power God. Bottom line, our fears are proportional to how we view God.

If our God is small, then our problems are big.
If our God is big, then our problems are small.

Therefore, when fear knocks at the door, we must ask ourselves: Is my God bigger than this situation? Can Jesus provide for my needs? Is God able to defeat my enemy? How we answer these questions is directly related to what we believe about Him. This is why A. W. Tozer said, "What comes into our minds when we think about God is the most important thing about us."

Imagine you were on the boat with the disciples, and you witnessed Jesus standing on the waves. What does this miracle reveal about His power and ability?

It's important to note that the ocean symbolized the uncontrollable and chaotic world to people in Biblical times. The sea represented the untamed darkness. The unpredictable nature of the waves and the great unknown of the deep spoke grave fear to people's hearts. Disorder, confusion, and terror entwined with enormous superstition that evil lurked below the waves.

Jesus' mastery over the sea is a miracle of multiple proportions: The sheer fact that He, a man, walks upon the water, is pretty stinking cool. We could stop there and stand amazed. We see that the natural forces of this world do not constrain Him. He is the Master of molecules. Jesus displays His glory by doing the impossible and, in doing so, confronts His disciple's desperate fears and ours, too.

To "walk upon" water reveals Christ's dominion, power, and authority. Recalling that the water symbolized chaos and evil to people, Jesus declares that He rules and reigns. The forces of darkness are not greater than our God.

With each masterful step upon the unruly waves, Jesus foreshadows His ultimate mission: to defeat Satan, to redeem humanity from the curse of sin, and to deliver us from the domain of darkness. And Jesus' perfect love for us casts out all fear! Paul Tripp explains why, because of Jesus, we can be free of fear:

> *Fear lives and rules in the heart of a believer who has forgotten God's sovereignty and grace. If left to myself, I should be afraid. There are many trials, temptations, dangers, and enemies in this fallen world that are bigger and more powerful than me. I have to deal with some things that are outside of my control. But the message of the Gospel is that I haven't been left to myself, that Immanuel is with me in sovereign authority and powerful grace. He rules with perfect wisdom over all the circumstances and locations that would make me afraid.*
> — *Paul David Tripp,* New Morning Mercies

Knowing that my God is able to tread over the seas, to silence the waves, and stop a storm fills me with confidence and hope.

- Hope that my God is greater than all forces of darkness that come against me.
- Hope that despite what I see around me, Jesus wins!
- Hope that reminds my fearful heart, "Nothing is impossible with God!"

Stop and marvel at Jesus, who is the Lord of all creation! Remember that nothing is impossible for Him. Release any fears and confess your worries to Jesus.

Day 2: John 6:22-71

Most Christ followers come to a place called the decision point. It is the moment when we make a choice: Will we continue to follow Jesus or not? I have witnessed these decision points countless times when meeting with women. It's a fork in the road. Will they continue to follow Jesus, or walk away? Granted, the departure may not be evident to others. They may still attend church, small groups, and volunteer—but their hearts are closed, and they stop pursuing Jesus on a personal level. For others, the decision point is more dramatic. They publicly disengage from church and depart from the faith.

I've had this conversation countless times, and it goes like this: A woman asks to talk to me about something going on in her life. She's experiencing heartbreak, disappointment, or suffering. (Please hear me; I am not for a second minimizing their pain; it is real and raw. My job is to listen, offer comfort, and pray for God's healing in their situations.)

But so often, these conversations expose something else occurring in the heart. Many of these women are facing a real temptation to walk away from Jesus because life did not turn out as they expected. The question looming for them is this: Will I continue to follow God when He hasn't done what I wanted Him to do, changed my situation, fixed my problem, or provided my desire? This is their decision point.

What I discern is the enemy at work behind the scenes causing doubt and attacking faith. Friends, trust me when I tell you from personal experience that there is a real enemy who takes advantage of our pain and tries to cause doubt about the goodness of God. This enemy, whom Jesus called the Father of Lies, is the one who wants us to stop following Jesus when life gets hard.

She could be a single woman who is mad at God because she's not married or an exhausted mom who is upset with God because her child is challenging. This conversation could be with an angry woman venting because her husband is cheating. All of these are valid causes of heartache. But behind each scenario brews an accusation—If God were good, then He wouldn't allow this to happen to me. That's the spirit of offense at work.

I share these conversations because our text today finds the massive crowds following Jesus at their own decision point. Will they continue to follow Him, or walk away? As we read the passage, we lean into the dialogue and hear the problem—the people came to Jesus with certain expectations. They want an earthly king, who would defeat the Roman oppressors, provide plenty of bread, and keep on performing cool miracles for them to see.

They wanted stuff from God, but they didn't want a relationship with God. Jesus sees to the heart of the matter. He knows the masses have only followed Him because of what they can get from Him (food and miracles) instead of because of who He is. Jesus knows this is not authentic faith. He understands that the crowd is missing the point—the most vital need is one that is spiritual, not physical.

Read John 6:22–59.

Note any titles Jesus uses to describe Himself.

Why did the crowds look for Jesus? What did they want from Him (verses 26, 30–31, 34)?

Think back to the miracle we beheld yesterday in John 6:1–15 (the feeding of the 5000). What kind of impression do you think this left on the people?

What radical claim does Jesus make about Himself in this conversation (verse 35, 51, 58)?

How do the crowds respond to Jesus' claim (verses 41–42, 52)?

As you read through today's passage, we hear Jesus proclaim, "I Am the Bread of Life." In the conversation, Jesus clearly tells the crowd that the manna in the wilderness simply foreshadowed the true bread that would one day come from heaven. Jesus makes the audacious claim that He is that bread.

To understand the implications of this passage, we must stop and ask why Jesus uses this metaphor to describe Himself. What exactly does He mean by the phrase, "I am the Bread of Life?"

Let's start by thinking of bread in the natural realm. God bless the people who invented King's Hawaiian Rolls. As we say in East Texas, that stuff is slap yo' momma good! But I digress; this carb-loving woman can easily get distracted by the thought of a breadbasket.

What's the point of Jesus' declaration that He is the Bread of Life? When you eat a piece of bread, the energy of the food is released (we call these calories). First, the bread is tasted in the mouth, swallowed, and then digestion begins. Then the nutrients circulate through the bloodstream and give power to the body. This is what happens when we consume bread in the natural realm—we are nourished and given energy for physical tasks.

Jesus uses this metaphor to illustrate His life in us. When we believe in Jesus, His Spirit comes to reside within us, and becomes part of our being. This "Bread" then transforms us from the inside out by releasing His power into our inner being. It circulates through us, providing new desire to please God, and the supernatural ability to break old sinful habits. We are nourished, empowered, and transformed because of this spiritual bread.

Note that Jesus calls Himself the Bread of "Life." The word "life" is essential to understanding His point. There are two Greek words for life. (We only have one in the English language.) The two Greek words are *bios* and *zoe*. *Bios* is the word for biological, physical life, but *zoe* is the word for the quality of life we experience: the everlasting and abundant life. When the crowds asked for bread, they wanted to satisfy the needs of *bios*, but Jesus always used the word *zoe* when He answered them.

Jesus is talking about another kind of bread that brings real *zoe*. As you and I know, there's a big difference between merely existing and thriving. The life Jesus offers is the one that brings love, joy, peace, patience, hope, faithfulness, self-control, and goodness (to name a few characteristics.) Jesus offers a radically different life than the one we experience when we don't digest the Bread of Heaven.

Jesus offers something that can't be purchased on Amazon; He offers something that will not rot in our pantry; He provides a life that will withstand the trials, storms, and setbacks that come with living in this broken and fallen world. Jesus wanted more for the crowds than they wanted for themselves. They were willing to settle for some stale saltines, when He wanted to give them Wonder Bread!

Let's look at the conclusion of this conversation, or what I call the decision point.

Read John 6:60–71.

What was the disciples' response to Jesus' invitation to eat the Bread of Life (verse 60)?

What question does Jesus ask them in verse 61?

Why do you think they are offended?

How does Jesus describe the words He spoke to them (verse 63)? What do you think this means?

As a result of this conversation, what happened to the crowds (verse 66)?

This scene is heartbreaking. I've known many people who have made this same choice. They followed Jesus for a season, but when a time of testing came, they walked away.

Friends, I've been there. When I was in my mid-thirties, I experienced a heartbreaking season. I was single, and the desire of my heart for marriage remained unmet. It seemed like God had forgotten me. Then I dated someone who I thought was "the one." And then when we broke up, I was devastated. Pain screamed in my ears, and the enemy of my soul took advantage of my heartbreak and tempted me with this question—if God is so good, why do you hurt so bad?

Decision point. Would I continue to follow Jesus even if my life didn't turn out how I hoped? Did I come to Jesus to get my plan for my life, or did I come to Jesus to get the abundant life? I wrestled. I agonized. My flesh said, "Walk away." But the Spirit inside of me held fast to the Bread of Life. Why? Because I had tasted and experienced the goodness of God, and I knew: Jesus is better.

I knew I'd never find real life apart from Jesus. The Apostle Peter and the other disciples came to the same conclusion—Jesus is better! Let's look at their decision point and hear why they chose to stick with Jesus.

Read John 6:67–71.

What question does Jesus ask His disciples (verse 67)?

How does Simon Peter answer (verse 68)?

Who does Peter identify Jesus to be (verse 69)?

As I close today's study, I sense we are on holy ground. Perhaps you are at a decision point. Life's hard and you're being tempted to walk away from Jesus. Or maybe, the pain is now a distant memory, but you can look back and see how a part of your heart hardened towards God. Wherever you are today, whether you are feasting on God's goodness or famished from turning from Him, I promise you that Jesus welcomes you with open arms. Run to Him. Confess your need for the abundant, *zoe*, life. Friend, I promise you this—Jesus is better!

Spend time talking to God about your heart. Use the space provide to be real, honest, and open with the One who already knows and sees and loves you anyway!

> Jesus answered, "My teaching is not my own. It comes from the one who sent me. Anyone who chooses to do the will of God will find out whether my teaching comes from God or whether I speak on my own."
> JOHN 7:16–17

Day 3: John 7:1-31

I often hear people say that time is our greatest commodity, especially in western cultures where the vast majority of us have our physical needs met. Most of us long for time more than we do other basic necessities. For example, we don't need to walk to a well each day to find clean water. Instead, we turn on a faucet. We don't plow the earth, plant seed, and pray for rain to put food on our tables. Instead, we drive through a fast-food restaurant and order our meals. While we have these luxuries in abundance, the one thing we don't have, and can't make more of, is time.

One of the wealthiest and most successful men in the modern

world, Steve Jobs, the founder of Apple, once said, "My favorite things in life don't cost any money. It's really clear that the most precious resource we have is time."

How true! We just blink, and our kids are graduating from high school. We look in the mirror and see the ravages of time marked on aging faces. We open our calendars to see days, weeks, and months filled with activities and deadlines that leave us feeling exhausted. The cliché "time flies" is a popular for a reason.

I want us to think about the concept of time because today, we will hear Jesus repeatedly mention the word. Jesus understands the importance of timing. He knows that He was born to fulfill a specific mission, and this assignment was prophesied for centuries before His birth in Bethlehem. Jesus is aware that all of the scriptures in the Old Testament point to Him, and these symbols are telling a story.

Bottom line, the date, time, and moment when Jesus fulfilled His mission as Savior of the World was not arbitrary. We hear Him say that it will not be left to the whims of man. Jesus is in control of His destiny, and He is fully surrendered to the Father's will. Therefore, His movements are intentional. Jesus knows there is an invisible clock counting down to His death. It will not happen one minute sooner or later than His Heavenly Father has planned.

Friend, God is in control, and God is in the details.

Before we dive into our further study of John, I want to share one of my all-time favorite verses, which helps us comprehend Jesus' understanding of His time and His destiny.

> *But when the fullness of the time came, God sent His Son, born of a woman, born under the Law, so that He might redeem those who were under the Law, that we might receive the adoption as sons and daughters. Because you are sons, God has sent the Spirit of His Son into our hearts, crying out, "Abba! Father!" Therefore you are no longer a slave, but a son; and if a son, then an heir through God.*
> *— Galatians 4:4–7*

WEEK 3

Read John 7:1–31.

Based on your initial reading, how would you describe the tone of these conversations?

Now go back and notice the repetition of Jesus' statements about time. What do verses 6, 8 and 30 reveal about Jesus' time?

This portion of John can easily be divided into three sections: *doubt, debate,* and *division*. First, we see the *doubt* of his biological brothers, who want Jesus to prove His identity. Next, we see the *debate* with the religious leaders about Jesus' authority to teach the people. Finally, we see that a *division* arises among the crowds as some put faith in Christ and others do not.

Review verses 1–9.

Why does Jesus want to remain in Galilee (verse 1)?

What do Jesus' biological brothers want Him to do (verses 3–4)?

Why does Jesus say the world "hates" Him (verse 7)?

Here we see His brothers' doubt on display. They dare Jesus to go to Jerusalem and show off and prove that He's the Messiah. They taunt Him and say, "show yourself!" Long before *Frozen 2* hit the

77

theatres, and Elsa sang the famous song, *Show Yourself*, Jesus' own brothers challenged Him to do the same.

Jesus has no desire to prove Himself to the world. He knows who He is and why He came. He performed miracles out of compassion and to meet people's needs, not to parade signs before skeptics. Plus, He knows that the "world," as His brothers describe it, hates Him. When Jesus refers to "the world," He is not referring to people, but rather to the world system (ruled by the enemy) that opposes and hates God. Jesus knows that this world system hates Him because He, the Light of the World, exposes the darkness in it. His love exposes hate. His sacrifice exposes selfishness. His truth exposes lies. The world does not want sin exposed, so it hates Jesus.

Finally, we see that Jesus' reason for denying their request goes back to the issue of time. He knows full well that the religious authorities in Jerusalem are looking for Him and awaiting an opportunity to kill Him. But, He also knows that the timing of His death must happen on the Feast of Passover (as we will see in a few weeks), and not on the Feast of Tabernacles. Therefore, He intentionally plans His schedule and makes His entry into Jerusalem when the time is right.

Review verses 10–24. Here we see a heated debate between Jesus and the Jews. (Note, this is John's term for the religious leadership.)

What are a couple things people are saying about Jesus (verses 12–13)?

Next, Jesus taught in the temple courts. This stirs up unrest with the religious leaders. What specifically do they want to know about Him in verse 15?

Where does Jesus claim His authority to teach comes from (verses 16–18)?

Finally, the debate returns to the issue of the law. The religious leadership is upset because they believes Jesus ignored God's law concerning the Sabbath regulations. (Although He didn't.) Jesus is actually correcting their misguided understanding of the Sabbath and showing how the strict legalism is putting a burden upon people that God never intended.

In verses 23–24, Jesus fires back with a brilliant response to their accusations. What does He say?

It's important to remember that these debates and teachings are happening in a public arena, in front of spectators. Some of these people have already witnessed Jesus' miracles, and some sat at His feet listening to Him illuminate scripture. From John's explanation, it seems that Jesus is the hot topic of conversation—and the question at hand is this: Is He the Messiah?

Now we come to the final section of today's text, the division. Here we see the people are divided into two groups on the question of Jesus: believers and non-believers.

Review verses 25–31.

Describe the two different positions concerning Jesus. Who do some people believe He is?

When the leaders attempt to arrest Him, what is John's explanation for why this didn't happen (verse 30)?

Friend, today we've seen the doubt, the debate, and the division that arose concerning Jesus. But amid all the scuffle, we also discovered that Christ fully understood His destiny. Jesus would not be pressured by family to perform miracles, He would not be intimidated by the so-called authorities, and the fickle opinions of people would not sway Him. Instead, Jesus understood His mission—to redeem humanity—and with eyes fixed on the cross, He presses on through the crowds to do His Father's will.

Conclude your time in God's word by praising Jesus, who did not allow the plots of man or schemes of darkness to alter His destiny.

Day 4: John 7:32-52

Yesterday we left our study at a cliff-hanger. Looming in the air was the million-dollar question—*Is Jesus the Messiah?* The crowds surrounding Him are divided into two camps. Some believe and some do not. The unbelievers are vicious in their opposition—they passionately want to arrest and kill Jesus. Yet, as we discovered, Jesus is in command. He knows the moment that He is destined to die. He is on a mission and will not be deterred until He fulfills every prophecy and promise concerning the Christ. Time is His servant, not His master.

Today we dive into one of my favorite passages in all of scripture. The waters (pun very intended) are deep and wide. This text is so rich that we will study it both today in our homework and in the next live Bible study.

The context of this passage is the same as yesterday. Jesus is in

Jerusalem for the Feast of Tabernacles and is teaching in the temple courts, where there is a mixed crowd consisting of followers and the religious authorities who want to silence Him.

Read John 7:32–52.

What do the Pharisees and Chief Priests attempt to do in verse 32?

Verses 37–39 are the focal point of our study today. What does Jesus promise to those who believe in Him?

John explains that the rivers of living water refer to the Spirit. Why had the Spirit not been given yet (verse 39)?

What conclusion do some come to concerning the identity of Jesus (verse 41)?

The temple guards who were assigned to arrest Jesus are unable to fulfill their mission. What reason do they give for their failure (verses 45–46)?

Who speaks up and defends Jesus in the face of the religious rulers (verse 50)?

The Feast of Tabernacles:
The purpose of the Feast of Tabernacles was to celebrate how God led the Israelites out of slavery in Egypt, through the wilderness, and into the Promised Land. This is their journey to freedom. Therefore, the entire heartbeat of the feast is to celebrate the emancipation from captivity and the cloud of God's presence that led them each step of the way.

> *Those in whom the Spirit comes to live are God's new Temple. They are, individually and corporately, places where heaven and earth meet.*
> — N.T. WRIGHT

Based on what you remember about Nicodemus (John 3), do you think he's in the camp of believers or non-believers?

What personal risk does Nicodemus face to his standing, power, and wealth at defending Jesus?

The Feast of Tabernacles began on a Sunday night and lasted for seven days. It was the seventh festival given to Israel and was rich with symbolism, which all pointed to Jesus. This feast is also called "Sukkot," the Hebrew word for booths or tents. So sometimes, you will hear it referred to as the Feast of Booths.

In the Old Testament, God instructed the Israelites to live in tents for seven days (Leviticus 23:42), and the tradition continues even to this day in modern Israel! This feast reminded the Israelites that God led them by His presence (a cloud by day and a fire by night) through the desert. As they lived in tents and progressed towards the Promised Land, the Lord provided for their every need (water, food, protection ... to name a few). But this feast ultimately pointed to a time when God would again "tabernacle" with His people. The restoration of His presence with them, a return to Eden, was the purpose of redemption.

Based on our reading today, we discover that Jesus uses this specific feast to reveal His messianic identity. Additionally, Jesus links belief in Him to a great promise given in the Old Testament concerning the outpouring of the Holy Spirit. These two revelations go hand in hand.

Central to this feast was the water libation ceremony, when the priests gathered a pitcher of water from the Pool of Siloam and poured it out on the altar inside the Temple. The pouring of the water served as a reminder of God's provision of water in the desert and expressed Israel's hope for future rains to produce an abundant harvest. Thus, this celebration wasn't only a cry for physical rain but a desperate cry that God would pour out his Spirit—the "living water" of His presence.

As we would imagine, God providing water in a barren desert for millions of people was a pretty big deal. Scholars note that the procession from the Pool of Siloam to the altar occurred in complete silence. This ceremony was held on the last day of the feast. John makes specific mention that it was at this precise moment that Jesus stands and says, "If anyone is thirsty, let him come to Me and drink!" (John 7:37)

Based on what we've learned about this Feast and what water symbolizes, what is Jesus implying with this invitation to "Come to Me and drink?"

What does Jesus mean by "thirsty?"

Thirst is a metaphor that illustrates our desperate need for God. To "drink" means to believe that Jesus alone quenches that thirst. Accepting this invitation is more than mere intellectual agreement with Jesus' identity. To drink implies to experience, to trust, and to depend upon Him. When we come to Jesus and drink the Living Water, we forsake other fountains, admitting that they will never truly satisfy our thirst. Trusting in Jesus for life is what it means to be a Christian. As C.S. Lewis once wrote:

> *All that we call human history—money, poverty, ambition, war, prostitution, classes, empires, slavery—the long, terrible story of man trying to find something other than God which will make him happy.*
> *–C. S. Lewis, Mere Christianity*

> *"Religion can reform a person's life, but it can never transform him. Only the Holy Spirit can transform."*
>
> — A.W. TOZER

The gift and the outpouring of the Holy Spirit, which is symbolized in the Feast of Tabernacles, is the restoration of God's presence with us. Without Jesus, the human condition is symbolized by a desperate thirst. We have all turned to various places to quench it, but ultimately nothing satisfies. Our souls need living water.

Jesus offers living water to those who turn to Him in faith. He makes it simple: if we believe, we receive.

Why do we need the Holy Spirit if Jesus forgives our sin? Because forgiveness of sin is not enough to cure the human condition; we require a new nature. This new nature is the Holy Spirit of God living within us.

We can't live abundant and victorious lives without His power. Bottom line, at the cross, Jesus forgives our sin, but at His resurrection, He gives us His strength (the Holy Spirit) to live in victory. That's why the apostle Paul said in Colossians 1:27, it "is Christ in you, the hope of glory." Therefore, our only hope to live glorious lives comes through the power of God living in us. All of us need the river of life flowing through us!

Christianity is not a self-improvement religion in which one tries harder to do better. On the contrary, a genuine follower of Jesus admits, "I can't do it. I need Jesus."

Our desperate need is the reason Jesus gives this invitation. He says, "if you believe, then you receive." When we come to the end of ourselves and recognize that we can't glorify God on our own, that is when we trust in Christ for our righteousness. By faith, we trust Jesus, and then He puts His Spirit within us, enabling us to live as lights in the darkness.

Stop and pray, "Jesus, I believe. I want to receive the fullness of Your Spirit." Open your heart to the Living Water and invite Him to quench your deepest thirst and flood your being with the Presence of God.

BEHOLD AND BELIEVE

Video Teaching Notes

Video teachings available for free at www.beholdandbelieve.com.

WEEK 4: BEHOLD, THE SON OF MAN

> No one has ever gone into heaven except the one who came from heaven—the Son of Man. Just as Moses lifted up the snake in the wilderness, so the Son of Man must be lifted up, that everyone who believes may have eternal life in him. — John 3:13–15

I. Jesus vs. Region

Religion says:

Jesus says:

> The Bible isn't a rule book. It's a love letter. I'm not an employee. I'm a child. It's not about my performance. It's about Jesus' performance for me. Grace isn't there for some future me but for the real me. The me who struggled. The me who was messy … He loves me in my mess; he was not waiting until I cleaned myself up. — Jefferson Bethke

Two questions the religious leaders consistently asked Jesus:

_____ do you think you are?
_____ gives you the right?

II. Jesus' Miracles Validated His Identity

- Jesus transforms water into wine — John 2:1–11
- Jesus heals the Nobleman's Son — John 4:46–54
- Jesus heals a Paralyzed Man — John 5
- Jesus feeds the 5,000 — John 6:5–15
- Jesus walks on water — John 6:16–21

- Jesus gives sight to a blind man — John 9:1–7
- Jesus raises Lazarus from dead — John 11:1–45

III. Jesus Heals the Paralyzed Man

The Miracle; John 5:1–15

The Confrontation; John 5:18–19

The Answer; John 5:24–29

IV. Why is Jesus called the "Son of Man"; Daniel 7:13–14

SMALL GROUP QUESTIONS

1. What did you behold about Jesus in your homework this week? What did this revelation lead you to believe?
2. What is the difference between Jesus and religion?
3. How did the miracles of Jesus validate His claims and teachings?
4. How is the paralyzed man a picture of all of us?
5. Why is the title "Son of Man" so significant to understanding who Jesus is?
6. Read Jesus' words in John 3:13–15. Considering the fact that the Hebrew people had to "look up" at the bronze serpent to be saved from physical death. What does this imply about faith or believing in Jesus for salvation?

WEEK 4

Day 1: John 8:1-12

I spent well over a decade of my life traveling to university campuses across the globe, telling young women about Jesus. So, if you need to know the best pizza place in Tuscaloosa or the best burger joint in Baton Rouge, I'm your girl. Thankfully, I did more than eat my way through the SEC; I had the incredible privilege of sharing the Gospel with many who believed the lie that they must be perfect to earn God's love. I also looked at the ones who were deep in shame and, with joy, told them that no one could out-sin the grace of God.

How did I get there? When I first surrendered my life to Christ, I knew one thing for certain—my life was not my own anymore. I belonged heart and soul to my Redeemer, and wherever He would lead, I would go! Little did I know that Jesus would lead me back to the very place where I had walked through the darkest sin of my own life. Sadly, my college days were marked by hookups and hangovers. Like many young women, I searched for love in all the wrong places. Unfortunately, all of this partying left me broken. That is, until I met Jesus.

When I was 25 years old, I heard the Gospel of Grace and walked out of the darkness to follow Jesus, the Light of the World. His mercy eclipsed my shame, and I fell head over heels in love with my Redeemer. When the Lord called me into full-time ministry, He first sent me back to college campuses to share my redemption story. Back then, I was still almost young enough to fit in, and I could relate to the temptations, the insecurities, and the searching that these young women faced. But more importantly, I knew the One who could set them free.

I traveled from north to south, east to west, telling college women about Jesus, and every single time, I shared the story we study today. On stage in basketball arenas, lecture halls, sorority houses, and collegiate theatres, I opened my Bible to John chapter 8. I shared how Jesus responded to a sinful woman who felt trapped and condemned because she had been looking for love in all the wrong places.

The context for today's focal passage is similar to our last study. Jesus is in Jerusalem, and the Feast of Tabernacles has just concluded. Now a great division exists among the people—there are two camps, believers and non-believers. Today, we see Jesus surrounded primarily by the latter. In this exchange, His opponents use despicable measures to try to discredit Jesus, but through it all we discover why Jesus is simply the best. There's no question, He has no rival!

Read John 8:1–12.

Where is Jesus when this confrontation occurs? Is this scene public or private?

What does verse 4 tell us the woman has been caught doing?

What do the "teachers of the law and the Pharisees" ask Jesus?

John indicates in verse 6 the appalling purpose for which these men were using this woman. What was their intent?

As a woman I have a strong and visceral reaction to this scene. The injustice of it strikes a nerve. After all, where in the world is the man who was committing the adultery with her? As the old saying goes, "It takes two to tango!" This trap reveals the depth of the jealousy and hypocrisy of the religious system of the time. Sure, adultery is wrong. It is a sin. No question. But there is a sinister plot at work, and that is the point of the story.

I greatly appreciate James Boice's explanation of this trap:

> First, the story reveals sin's horror. And, of course, I do not mean the sin of the woman. I mean the sin of the rulers. Adultery is sin, certainly. The woman was guilty of adultery. But compared to the sin of the men who were using her in an attempt to trap Jesus, her sin was minimal. To understand precisely what these men were doing we must understand that not only was their approach to Jesus a trap; they actually had already been active in trapping the woman.
>
> Under Jewish law, as it was practiced by the rabbis in the time of Christ and later, it was necessary to have multiple witnesses to the act of intercourse before the charge of adultery could be substantiated. Under these conditions the obtaining of evidence in adultery would be almost impossible were the situation itself not a setup. We are justified in supposing that the liaison had been arranged, perhaps by the very man who committed adultery with the woman. Was he a member of the Sanhedrin? Whatever the case, the arrangement must have involved the posting of witnesses in the room or at the keyhole.[21]

To fully understand this scene, we must see it for what it is: a setup. The leaders used one of their own to seduce a woman and then watched (like creepers) to verify that adultery occurred. Then with brazen hypocrisy they dragged her into the temple courts to stand at the feet of Jesus.

What do they claim the law instructs them to do with the woman (verse 5)?

Using your imagination, how do you think the woman felt, surrounded by the crowds and facing the possibility of death by stoning?

> "Grace means there is nothing I can do to make God love me more, and nothing I can do to make God love me less. It means that I, even I who deserve the opposite, am invited to take my place at the table in God's family."
>
> PHILIP YANCEY, WHAT'S SO AMAZING ABOUT GRACE?

Fear, shame, helplessness, and hopelessness are a few words that come to mind when I put myself in the sandals of this woman. She's facing certain death and a horrible one at that. She will be stoned, all at the hands of the very men who set up her entrapment.

I submit to you this thought—what we are witnessing here is a trial. The woman is not on trial for adultery; instead, Jesus is on trial to determine whether or not He is truly the Messiah. The rulers know that the real Messiah would never forsake God's law and let sin go unpunished, but they also knew Jesus' ministry was marked by compassion. So the question on the table is this: How will Jesus respond to this woman? With mercy or with justice? With grace or with the truth?

I'll be honest, this scene, this moment of sheer brilliance that fully reveals the heart of God and the hypocrisy of religion, is one of the reasons I fell in love with Jesus. So let's look at how He shut down this circus and brought light into the darkness.

Read Jesus' response in John 8:6–11.

What physical act does Jesus do in verse 6?

What challenge does He give the crowd in verse 7?

> "He made Him who knew no sin to be sin on our behalf, so that we might become the righteousness of God in Him."
> 2 CORINTHIANS 5:2

What was the crowd's response to Jesus' challenge (verse 9)?

Write down the full question that Jesus asked the woman who stood accused (verse 10).

According to verse 11, does Jesus show her justice or mercy?

What challenge does He give the woman in verse 11? Is this truth or grace?

Here's the rich irony: the only sinless person who ever lived was Jesus Christ. The religious leaders had no right to judge this woman, but Jesus had every right, and His judgment was true. Unfortunately, the religious leaders underestimated Jesus' divine wisdom and how He could see through their charade and get to the heart of the matter.

Most scholars debate what Jesus did when He stooped to the ground and wrote with His finger. Some speculate that He listed the names of every accuser, proving that He was all-knowing. Some say He scribbled their specific sins, revealing that they too stood guilty.

I think Jesus simply wrote the Ten Commandments—God's holy law. I don't know for certain, but I believe He bent down and wrote:

You shall have no other gods before me.
You shall honor your father and mother.
You shall not lie.
You shall not steal.
You shall not covet.

And yes, you shall not commit adultery.

And after this gesture, He made a simple statement: "Let any of you who is without sin be the first to throw a stone at her." Jesus knew their hearts and exposed their darkness. Not one person standing in judgment could claim to be without sin. Each would have to look at the Ten Commandments and honestly confess they had broken God's holy law in some form or fashion. Each person holding a stone knew that he needed grace just as much as this woman did, and with that revelation, they dropped their stones and walked away.

If we were to leave the story at this juncture, we would make a grave miscalculation about Jesus. Many end their reading here and assume He doesn't care about sin and simply winks at the woman's adultery. This is not the case. While He shows her incredible mercy, He also speaks to her a clear word of truth: "Go and leave your life of sin."

Jesus gets to the heart of the matter for both parties. For the religious hypocrites, He exposes their deception, and they leave with their tails between their legs. But with the woman, He sees her heart as well. She believed the lie that a man would fill the God-shaped hole in her soul for love and validation. Unfortunately, this led to a life of sin. Jesus loved her too much to let her remain there, so He called her to repentance.

Repentance means to turn. It means to head in a different direction. Jesus cared too deeply for this woman's well-being to turn a blind eye to the darkness she was in. No, He called her out of the darkness and into His marvelous light.

Now, let's conclude this study by looking at the "I Am" statement Jesus makes on the heels of this encounter.

Write John 8:12.

Why do you think Jesus uses this metaphor (light) to describe Himself in this situation?

When I heard the Gospel in my early twenties, I knew I desperately needed God's grace. I was thirsty for forgiveness and wholeness. But I needed God's truth too. I needed His truth to set me free from the bondage to sin. The call to follow Jesus is one where we leave our old lives and follow our Redeemer. When I came to Jesus, I experienced the same mercy that the woman caught in adultery experienced and heard the same call: Go and sin no more. I knew I had to leave behind the lifestyle of sexual sin, drunkenness, and debauchery. Why? Because that life was of the darkness, and I belonged to the one who is the Light of the World.

Read Ephesians 5:8 and 1 Thessalonians 5:5. What call are we given as Christ followers?

Friend, Jesus shines into our darkness both grace and truth. We all need God's mercy, but we also need His truth that sets us free. Talk to Jesus about any sin in your heart and ask for the forgiveness that He lavishly provides.

Day 2: John 8:13-58

Yesterday we ended our study with a thud. Literally. We concluded with the sound of stones hitting the ground. Stones that were intended to kill a woman were thrown down as Jesus confronted the religious leaders with their hypocrisy. One by one, they dropped their stones and walked away. Today, those same men will pick up those stones again, but this time Jesus is their target.

Today's focal passage feels like watching a tennis match. It's a back-and-forth debate between Jesus and the religious establishment. My goal is to break it down, "serve by serve," so we can better understand the significance of Jesus' claims and why they are intent on killing Him. Stick with this one; there is a dramatic conclusion to this match!

What dramatic claim does Jesus make in John 8:12 (see margin)?

> *When Jesus spoke again to the people, he said, "I am the light of the world. Whoever follows me will never walk in darkness, but will have the light of life."*
> JOHN 8:12

To grasp Jesus' opponents' shock and awe, we need to understand the context. Recall that Jesus is in Jerusalem for the Feast of Tabernacles. As we've discovered, this feast celebrated how God led His people through the wilderness journey and provided for all their needs. Thus, Jesus' invitation for the thirsty to come to Him and drink referred to God's provision of water in the desert. Now we see that His claim to be the Light of the World is also directly tied to the Feast of Tabernacles.

After sunset on the first night of the feast, two great lamps were lit in the temple courts. These cast their light over every quarter of the city. The lamps symbolized the pillar of cloud and fire that had accompanied the people in their wilderness wanderings. This light was the cloud of God's presence. The light first appeared when the people left Egypt: it stood between the Israelites and the pursuing armies of the Egyptians at the Red Sea.

Read Exodus 13:21–22; Exodus 40:34; 2 Chronicles 5:14 and describe what you learn about this cloud.

Why was the cloud important? It symbolized God's presence with His people. It is this cloud that Jesus referred to when He said, "I am the Light of the world." This audacious statement causes the great debate we read today. Now, let's watch the verbal tennis match that takes place between Jesus and His critics.

Read John 8:13–20.

What specific accusation do they lob at Jesus in verse 13?

It was Jewish custom that any testimony had to be validated by at least two witnesses. These leaders accuse Jesus of falsely claiming to be the Messiah because He doesn't have anyone to validate His claim.

Jesus responds by saying He does indeed have two witnesses. Who are they (verse 18)?

Jesus knew that His miracles validated that He was sent from the Father. One scholar makes this observation, "Jesus knew his origin and his destiny. In other words, Jesus knows God the Father, and the words that Jesus spoke were from the Father himself."[22]

To this, the Jews ask, "Where is your father?" How does Jesus respond to this question (verse 19)?

Although the leaders have wanted to arrest and kill Jesus this entire time, why does John indicate that this plan does not succeed (verse 20)?

Now the Pharisees begin to belittle and insult Jesus on a personal level. What seems like a simple question, "Where is your father," is actually a personal slam at Jesus' mother. Many rumored that Mary had committed sexual sin and conceived Jesus. While scripture tells of Jesus' virgin birth (Luke 1–2) and His divine nature (John 1), the leadership accused Him of being bastard, or of illegitimate circumstances. This slur becomes evident in their statement later "We are not illegitimate children" (v. 41).[23]

Read John 8:21–30.

What question do they ask him in verse 25?

This question is an insult. The tone indicates, "You're a nobody." Here the pride and self-righteousness of His accusers is on display. They feel morally, intellectually, and socially superior to this man from the backwoods of Israel. Essentially, they say, "We own this place. Who does Jesus think He is to march into Jerusalem and shake things up?"

What promise does Jesus make in John 8:24?

Concerning this promise, one scholar notes:

> *Jesus replied to the scorn of the Pharisees by the truth that if they would not believe on him as their Messiah then they would die in their sins (vv. 21, 24). To die in sin means to die with the burden of one's sin upon oneself and, as a result, to be forced to bear the penalty of sin, which is spiritual death. God says that "the wages of sin is death" (Romans 6:23). Physical death is the separation of the soul and the spirit from the body. Spiritual death is the separation of the soul and the spirit from God. To die in sin is to die separated from God and to remain so forever.*[24]

The entire mission and ministry of Jesus is to save people from this reality. Sadly, the rejection of the Jewish leaders is a rejection of God's grace.

What promise does Jesus make in John 8:28–29?

Here Jesus speaks about His own death, when He would be "lifted up" on the cross. One commentary makes this point, "The Jews in Jesus' day understood the expression lifted up to signify crucifixion. That the religious leaders would realize who Jesus was does not mean that they would believe in him. Rather, it means that Jesus' claims would be proven through the Crucifixion and Resurrection."[25] When He is lifted up from the grave all His claims will be validated!

Read John 8:31–38.

With this background in mind, what do you think Jesus meant with the promise He made in John 8:32?

How do the Jewish leaders respond to this promise (verse 33)? Based on what you know of Jewish history, is their answer true or false?

Now see Jesus' response in verses 34–38. What promise does Jesus give (verse 36)? What kind of freedom does He offer?

Now we come to the last round of this verbal tennis match. Jesus and His critics close in on the central point. Jesus came to offer grace, life, freedom, and a relationship with the Father to any who would put their hope and faith in Him. This faith is not just an intellectual agreement with certain facts, but also a confident trust in Jesus as the only remedy to sin's problem.

Hope is where the rubber meets the road with Jesus' critics. Their confidence is in their ancestry. They falsely believe they are "right with God" because they are Abraham's offspring. It's like a teenager who told me that she was a Christian because her grandmother attended church all the time.

In this final dialogue we hear Jesus explain to them that it is not their DNA code that makes them righteous before God, and that they require the new birth into God's family, just like everyone else.

Read John 8:39–59 and see the dramatic conclusion to this debate.

Jesus' opponents placed their hope in the fact that they were descendants of Abraham. What would be an equivalent today? What might someone hope in for salvation that is just as empty?

What question do the Jews ask Jesus in verse 57?

What is Jesus' stunning reply in verse 58?

What did the Jews do upon hearing Him utter these words (verse 59)?

> *Moses said to God, "Suppose I go to the Israelites and say to them, 'The God of your fathers has sent me to you,' and they ask me, 'What is his name?' Then what shall I tell them?" God said to Moses, "I am who I am. This is what you are to say to the Israelites: 'I am has sent me to you.'"*
>
> EXODUS 3:13–14

Don't ever let anyone tell you that Jesus never claimed to be God. Right here, He makes the most blatant declaration to His divinity. By evoking the Holy Name, "I Am." Jesus told His opponents that He was God in the flesh.

Remember, the only other time the phrase "I Am" was used was Exodus 3:14, where God (in speaking to Moses at the burning bush) used that very phrase as His name. No identity statement could be more precise. This time, the Jews do not respond with more words, questions, or accusations. Instead, they pick up stones to kill Him for blasphemy. But once again, Jesus evades their plot, because His time had not yet come!

Ponder the fact that the same God who led His people with a cloud by day and a fire by night took on human form. Jesus is Emmanuel, God with us. Spend some time in prayer and worship, giving glory to the Great I Am!

Day 3: John 9

While taking seminary courses in Oxford, England one summer, I had the immense privilege of touring locations important to Christian history. One such site was the church of the great John Newton. If you are unfamiliar with his name, I promise you are not unfamiliar with his famous hymn "Amazing Grace."

John Newton penned the words of the beloved song as a testimony to the work Christ did in his life. Newton was radically rescued from the grip of sin, cleansed by the blood of Jesus, and boldly proclaimed to the world that God's grace was strong enough to set any captive free!

Newton should know, because he was a former slave trader. Let's not mince words here. John Newton captained a slave ship that profited from the selling of human beings. He was guilty of kidnapping, enslaving, degrading, torturing, and selling people who were made in the image of God.

His story is one that proves God can awaken the hardest heart and make that person a new creation for His glory! John Newton repented of the evil he'd committed and went on to be one of the biggest champions and fighters for the abolishment of slavery.

Until he died at the age of 82, John Newton never ceased to marvel at the grace of God that transformed him so completely. Shortly before his death he proclaimed during a sermon, "My memory is nearly gone, but I remember two things: That I am a great sinner, and that Christ is a great Savior!"[26]

"Amazing Grace" stands today as the most-recognized, and get this, the most-recorded song on the planet. Take a minute to read through the lyrics.

> *Amazing Grace, how sweet the sound*
> *That saved a wretch like me*
> *I once was lost, but now am found*
> *Was blind but now I see*
>
> *'Twas Grace that taught my heart to fear*
> *And Grace my fears relieved*
> *How precious did that Grace appear*
> *The hour I first believed*
>
> *Through many dangers, toils and snares*
> *We have already come*
> *'Twas Grace that brought us safe thus far*
> *And Grace will lead us home*
>
> *Amazing Grace, how sweet the sound*
> *That saved a wretch like me*
> *I once was lost but now am found*
> *Was blind but now I see*

Take a closer look at that last line—"was blind, but now I see!" This is Newton's testimony. While he didn't suffer from physical blindness, he did suffer from a spiritual one. Newton lifts this phrase directly from the lips of a man who was radically healed from blindness by Jesus Christ. But like the man we will study in today's focal passage, Newton experienced a miracle too—Jesus opened his eyes and gave him a new life: a life that was 100% due to the grace of God.

Today we dive into John 9—one of my favorite sections of scripture! This chapter presents the sixth sign (or miracle) recorded by John to validate Christ's deity. Don't forget, Jesus frequently performed miracles in order to meet human needs. But He also used miracles as a catalyst to convey spiritual truths and educate His disciples. This miracle does both.

The man we meet in this chapter was born blind; he had never seen the beauty of God's creation, he'd never watched a sunset, and he'd never beheld the face of his mother. If you are able to read this text, then like me, you can't imagine the power and miracle of eyesight. The gift of sight is something most of us take for granted. But for those who were born blind or for those who have lost their vision, they can greatly appreciate the magnitude of this miracle. It is not an exaggeration to say this work of God transformed everything, absolutely everything, for the man Jesus healed.

Read John 9.

What question do the disciples ask Jesus about the blind man (verses 1–2)?

What is Jesus' response to their question (verses 3–5)?

I'm going to preach for just a second. There is an unbiblical concept called Karma that has grown in popularity in the past few decades.

Karma is a Hindu/Buddhist teaching that essentially says that one's present-day suffering is due to some past mistake or decision. A more precise definition says it is the sum of a person's actions in previous states of existence, which are viewed as deciding their fate in future existences.

I call this concept unbiblical because Jesus declared it false. When the disciples ask the Lord about the cause of the man's blindness, they want to know whose sin (past failure, mistake, or action) caused the man's suffering. Jesus refuted this idea completely.

We live in a fallen world where suffering is a reality until the day that God makes all things new. We don't live in the paradise that God intended for us in Eden. We live in a world where babies die, cancer spreads, and tragedy strikes. It is horrific to lay the blame at the parents' feet or on the one enduring the sickness. Jesus doesn't do that, and neither should we.

For those suffering in this present world, this miracle shines as a beacon of hope, that God will make "all things" new (Revelation 21:5). God is in the restoration business. Just as Jesus restored the sight of the man born blind, so too, He redeems this broken world and will one day restore us to our Edenic state—where there is no more suffering, sorrow, or pain. This miracle is a glimmer of our future hope, of what can be in Christ.

How did Jesus heal the man born blind (verses 6–7)?

"Then the LORD God formed a man from the dust of the ground and breathed into his nostrils the breath of life, and the man became a living being."
GENESIS 2:7

Some scholars speculate that Jesus' use of clay was symbolic and pointed back to the Garden of Eden, when God created man from the dust of the earth (Genesis 2:7). This healing was a sign that revealed the New Creation that Jesus brings through redemption. This man was born blind. He didn't need healing of his old eyes; he required the gift of new eyes. The same is true of us; Jesus doesn't come to repair us. He comes to make us new creations. (2 Corinthians 5:17)

Read John 9:8–23 and describe how the various groups responded to this miracle:

The neighbors

The Pharisees

The parents

The man himself

The religious leaders had let it be known that anyone who confessed Jesus as the Christ would be cast out of the synagogue (v. 22). Excommunication for a Jewish family meant losing friends and family and all the benefits of their faith. It was this threat that forced the blind man's parents and neighbors to evade the Pharisees' questions, telling them to ask the man directly how he was healed.

This chapter contains some of the funniest dialogue in the Bible as the freshly healed man is brought before the religious leaders to give an account of his newfound eyesight. This interrogation proves who is truly blind in this situation—the ones who refuse to see that Jesus is the Messiah sent from God to save the world.

Read John 9:24–34.

What is the man's simple testimony (verse 25)?

What conclusion does the man make about Jesus in verse 33?

What consequence did he face for this testimony (verse 34)?

This man's testimony was simple. "I was blind, but now I see." Using your own "before and after," how would you state your own testimony in a few words?

Read the conclusion to this miracle in John 9:35–40.

Who does Jesus reveal Himself to be in verses 35–37? (See the Word Study: Son of Man for more details)

How does the man respond to this revelation (verse 38)?

> **Son of Man:**
> A title for the Messiah and one of Jesus' favorite titles used to describe Himself. The term points to the humanity and servanthood of Christ, but also reflects the prophetic vision in Daniel 7:13, where the Son of Man was given dominion, glory, and an everlasting kingdom.

Here we see such irony. The religious leaders remain blind. Their spiritual blindness and hardness of heart keep them from seeing who Jesus truly is. Yet, this man who was born physically blind is the one who can see clearly. The man sees that Jesus is sent from God and is the long-awaited Messiah (Son of Man). As a result, he puts faith in Him and bows down to worship. I find it fascinating that this is the only place in this Gospel where anyone is said to worship Jesus.[27] His worship of Jesus replaced his worship in the synagogue. He was rejected by men, but Jesus welcomed him home.

I'll never forget when Jesus opened my eyes to truly see. Before my salvation, I walked around in spiritual blindness. Blind to my own condition. Blind to God's splendor and glory. Blind to the obvious signs that point to a Creator. I can vividly recall the early days when He restored my spiritual sight. Finally, I saw my desperate need for grace and beheld the wondrous cross that paid the penalty for my sin. Before, I was blind to God's work in the world, but then everywhere I turned, I saw Divine fingerprints —the beauty of a sunrise, the miracle of a mother's womb, and the intelligent design of the human body. All creation points to the Creator. I didn't have eyes to see these things before, but when Jesus opened my heart to know Him, He gave me eyes to behold His glory. And like the blind man, I worshipped the One who gave me sight!

Conclude today's time in the Word with prayer. Spend some time in worship and giving glory to God for the many things that you see that reveal His splendor and majesty.

Day 4: John 10

I heard a great story once about an Australian man who faced criminal charges. He was arrested for stealing sheep. While this isn't a case that usually makes the evening news cycle, the outcome proved so remarkable that it made national headlines.

The accused man fervently denied the accusation of theft, claiming that the sheep were his own and had been missing for days. When the case finally went to court, the judge heard both sides of the argument but was unsure how to rule. So finally, the judge asked that the sheep be brought into the courtroom.

Then, the judge made a brilliant move. He ordered the accuser to go outside and call for the animal. In response, the sheep looked frightened and scurried away. Next, the judge told the defendant to go to the courtyard and call the sheep. When the accused man did so, the sheep ran toward him. The sheep recognized the very familiar voice of the shepherd—the one who had cared, provided, and protected it for many years. There was no fear in the sheep, but perfect trust and obedience to the call.

This story is a perfect example of the truth Jesus teaches us in John 10. He is our Good Shepherd! It's important to note the context of this teaching. In John 9, Jesus healed a man who was born blind. As a result of this miracle, the religious authorities kicked the man out of the synagogue because of his faith. Jesus uses the man rejected by religion to illustrate the true nature of a relationship with God. This relationship is symbolized by the relationship between sheep and a Good Shepherd who deeply cares for our needs. Jesus wants us to know that His sheep will never be taken from His fold!

Read John 10:1–21.

How does Jesus describe a relationship between sheep and a shepherd in verses 1–6?

What claim does Jesus make in verses 7 and 9?

Warren Wiersbe shares this helpful explanation about shepherding at the time of Christ:

> *The Middle Eastern sheepfold was very simple: a stone wall, perhaps ten feet high, surrounded it, and*

an opening served as the door. The shepherds in the village would drive their sheep into the fold at nightfall and leave the porter to stand guard. In the morning each shepherd would call his own sheep, which would recognize their shepherd's voice and come out of the fold. The porter (or one of the shepherds) would sleep at the opening of the fold and actually become "the door." Nothing could enter or leave the fold without passing over the shepherd.[28]

What warning does Jesus give about the thief in verse 10?

What promise does Jesus make about Himself in verse 10?

What claim does Jesus make in verses 11 and 14? (What specific action does the shepherd do for the sheep?)

Write out verses 14–15.

What does Jesus promise to do for His sheep?

Thoughtfully review verse 16. (Remember, Jesus is speaking to the religious leaders and His disciples, who are all ethnic Jews and practicing the Jewish religion.) Who do you think Jesus is referring to with this statement?

What does Jesus explain about His own death in verses 16–17?

What transpired among the crowds as a result of Jesus' statements (verses 19–21)?

The events in this next section occur about two and a half months after those described in John 10:1–21. John put them together because in both messages, Jesus used the imagery of the shepherd and the sheep. Once again, the leaders surround Jesus in the temple so that He has to stop and listen to them. They had decided that it was time for a "showdown" and they did not want Him to evade the issue any longer. "How long are You going to hold us in suspense," they keep saying to Him. "Tell us plainly—are You the Messiah?"[29]

Read John 10:22–42.

What reason does Jesus give to the religious leaders for their unbelief (verse 26)?

List every promise Jesus makes about His sheep in verses 27–29.

What comfort do the words of Christ give you about your place in God's family?

> *"Our Lord made a statement that He knew would startle His enemies and give them more reason to oppose Him (John 10:30). It was the "plain answer" that the religious leaders had asked for. "I and My Father are One" is as clear a statement of His deity as you will find anywhere in Scripture. This was even stronger than His statement that He had come down from heaven (John 6) or that He existed before Abraham ever lived." (John 8:58)*
>
> — WARREN WIERSBE

As we review Jesus' teaching about His identity as the Good Shepherd, we see three important aspects to His relationship with His sheep.

- First, Jesus has a loving relationship because He willingly dies for the sheep.
- Second, this is a *living* relationship because He cares for us. He is the Lord, the Good Shepherd who leads, guides, and provides for His sheep.
- Finally, we see that this is a lasting relationship. Jesus promises eternal life and that no one can snatch us from His hand. He is the Good Shepherd that guarantees that none of His are lost.

What bold claim does Jesus make in verse 30?

Once again, how do the Jews respond to this claim (verses 31–39)?

As we conclude our study today, I want us to pause and reflect on the promise Jesus makes to us, His sheep, in John 10:10. He promises an "abundant life" to the sheep in His care. This promise is beautifully depicted in the description of the Lord found in Psalm 23.

> *The Lord is my shepherd, I lack nothing.*
> *He makes me lie down in green pastures,*
> *he leads me beside quiet waters,*
> *he refreshes my soul.*
> *He guides me along the right paths*
> *for his name's sake.*
> *Even though I walk*
> *through the darkest valley,*
> *I will fear no evil,*
> *for you are with me;*

*your rod and your staff,
they comfort me.*

*You prepare a table before me
in the presence of my enemies.
You anoint my head with oil;
my cup overflows.
Surely your goodness and love will follow me
all the days of my life,
and I will dwell in the house of the Lord forever.
— Psalm 23*

How does this Psalm describe the "abundant life" Jesus promises us as our Good Shepherd?

Conclude your time in God's Word today by talking to Jesus, the Good Shepherd. Tell Him where you need guidance, provision, rest, or grace. He is the God who watches over you, cares for you, and laid down His life to die for you!

Video Teaching Notes

Video teachings available for free at www.beholdandbelieve.com.

WEEK 5: BEHOLD, THE GIVER OF LIFE

Jesus said, "If you believed Moses, you would believe Me; for He wrote of Me." — John 5:46

I. Two Keys Marked Israel's Wilderness Experience

The _____ of the Lord.
Exodus 13:21, Numbers 9:15–18, Exodus 33:14–16

The _____ of the Lord.
Exodus 15:22–27, Deuteronomy 8:1–4

The wilderness season was a time to learn _____ rather than self-reliance. The Israelites had to look to the Lord for their every need: food, water, shelter, and protection.

II. Jesus is God with Us

The Word became flesh and made His dwelling among us. We have seen His glory, the glory of the one and only Son, who came from the Father, full of grace and truth. — John 1:14

III. The Feast of the Lord

God appointed 7 feasts on the Hebrew calendar that required His people to come to Jerusalem 3 times per year to celebrate them. Each feast pointed to Jesus and are full fled by Him. The Feasts of the Lord are described in Leviticus 23 and critical to understanding John's Gospel.

The Feast of Passover (early spring)

The Feast of Pentecost (50 days after Passover)

The Feast of Tabernacles (fall or harvest time)

IV. Jesus and the Feast of Tabernacles

During the Feast of Tabernacles, God commanded His people to _____ and remember His presence and provision in their wilderness journey.

John's Gospel records that Jesus not only celebrated this festival, but took traditional elements of the festival and applied them to His life and ministry.

Jesus, the Living Water; John 7:37–39

Jesus, the Light of the World; John 8:12

SMALL GROUP QUESTIONS

1. What did you behold about Jesus in your homework this week? What did this revelation lead you to believe?
2. In today's teaching, Marian shared about the Israelite's wilderness experience. She said a wilderness is when we learn "God reliance" instead of "self- reliance." Read Deuteronomy 8:1–18 and then share a time when you learned to trust or rely on God for strength, provision, direction, or help.
3. How did Jesus fulfill the symbols in the Feast of Tabernacles?
4. Read John 7:37–38. What does Jesus invite us to do? How does the physical human condition of thirst point to the spiritual need for God?
5. Another name given to Jesus was Emmanuel, which means God with Us. How is this name appropriate given what you learned about the Feast of Tabernacles.
6. How does Jesus' interaction with the woman accused of adultery impact how you see Christ and His ministry?

WEEK 5

Day 1: John 11:1-52

Today I'm on a long road trip with my family from our home in Texas to the beautiful beaches of Seaside, Florida. This trip has been planned for nearly a year. We are going in honor of my mother-in-law, Patty Ellis, who deeply loved the ocean. She always said it was her happy place. So, we are headed to white sand and blue water to celebrate her life.

Patty passed away last summer after a 10-year battle with breast cancer. By the time she was diagnosed, cancer had spread to her bones and organs. I've never met a tougher woman in my life. Round after round of chemo, clinical trials, and radiation, and not once did I ever hear a complaint leave her lips. She fought hard. And for a season, it seemed like she won.

But in the end, the horrific illness took its toll. Last summer, we sat by her side as she entered the final stages of life. The weeks of hospice care blur together, like the tears that filled our eyes. There are no words to describe the anguish of those final days.

Amid the prayers for healing and pleas for mercy, one aspect of our faith came to the forefront—the promise of eternal life in Christ. When one walks through the valley of the shadow of death, what you believe about Jesus and the resurrection truly comes into focus.

Today, as we open the Gospel of John, we hear Jesus make another bold "I Am" statement. In my opinion, this one is the most audacious. And how we respond to His claim is indeed a matter of life and death for us.

Since sin and death entered the world in the Garden of Eden, humanity has cried out in grief for relief from its clutches. From battlefields to hospital beds, we've longed for a Redeemer to rescue us from our ultimate enemy.

And after years of waiting, watching, praying, and hoping, the One who came to conquer sin and death stepped into the human story. He robed Himself in our mortality. His name is Jesus, and He is the Redeemer for which all of humanity has longed.

In our study today, we see Jesus confront our enemy and reveal His unrivaled power over death. John's eyewitness testimony of watching Jesus raise Lazarus from the dead is the climactic miracle of this Gospel. It is the 7th and final sign that reveals Jesus' identity as the Messiah, and is the pivotal event that sets in motion the plot to put Jesus to death.

Read John 11:1–52.

How many times is "believe," "believing," or "believed" in this story?

Why is the key word "believe" so important?

Review John 11:1–6.

What does Jesus say would happen because of Lazarus' illness (verse 4)?

What does John reveal about Jesus' relationship with Lazarus and his sisters (verse 5)?

Putting ourselves in Mary and Martha's sandals, it's easy to imagine their fears. However, they know Jesus is a healer, and the sisters fix their hope on Him. They send messengers to Judea to let the Messiah know of the desperate situation.

How long does Jesus wait before going to help Lazarus (verse 6)?

It seems Jesus intentionally delays. Have you ever prayed for something and had to wait for an answer to your prayer? How do you think Mary and Martha felt as they waited for Jesus to arrive?

God's ways are not our ways. It's hard for us to comprehend why Jesus didn't hurry to Lazarus' aid. We question in our hearts, "Surely, if He loved him, Jesus would rush to the scene." But here's the thing about God—He sees and knows what we do not. He is orchestrating a sovereign plan that our finite minds cannot understand. Jesus specifically tells the disciples that the illness is for God's glory. While Mary and Martha can't comprehend the delay while it is occurring, they certainly behold the glory of God.

Review John 11:7–16.

How did the disciples respond to Jesus' desire to return to Judea (the village of Bethany)?

Read John 11:17–27.

What is Martha's attitude toward Jesus when He arrives?

What promise does Jesus make to her (verse 23)?

What "I Am" statement does Jesus make to Martha (verse 25)?

What proves the vital key to experiencing this resurrection (verses 25–26)?

What is Martha's confession of faith (verse 27)?

Read John 11:28–37.
What is Mary's posture and attitude towards Jesus (verse 32)?

How does Jesus respond to Mary's grief (verses 33–35)?

"Jesus wept" is the shortest verse in the Bible, yet it overflows from the heart of a compassionate, tender, and merciful God. Christ's response to Lazarus' death also reveals both His human and divine nature. Up to this point, He was in command, assuring Martha that her brother would rise because He was the "resurrection and the life." But when Mary appears, broken and weeping, we see Jesus overcome with profound emotion. His grief is described by the phrase "deeply moved," which in the original language means "to snort like a horse." This phrase generally connotes anger. It certainly is not irritation with the sisters. Instead, this expresss His passionate anger against the ravages of death that had entered our world because of sin. As a result, John beautifully states, "Jesus wept."

How does your heart respond to the image of Jesus' anger at death and grieving over your pain?

How did the Jews respond to Jesus' grief (verses 36–37)?

Read John 11:38–44.
Why does Martha protest when Jesus asks for the stone to be moved (verse 39)?

After praying, what simple command does Jesus utter to resurrect Lazarus (verse 43)?

In verse 40, Jesus reminds Martha of His earlier promise that if she believed she would see the glory of God. And now, with three simple words, her faith becomes sight! St. Augustine once said that if Jesus had not said Lazarus' name all would have come out from the graves. I love how *The Expositor's Bible Commentary* explains this miracle:

> The creative power of God reversed the process of corruption and quickened the corpse into life. The effect was startling ... It was a supreme demonstration of the power of eternal life that triumphed over death, corruption, and hopelessness.[30]

Read John 11:45–52 and note the two different responses to this miracle.

This miracle results in the Sanhedrin (the Jewish ruling council) meeting to decide once and for all what to do with Jesus. Their frustration at His growing prominence and popularity reaches a boiling point. One Bible commentary makes this observation:

> *They anticipated that the miracles of Jesus would bring such a wave of popular support that the Romans, fearing a revolution, would intervene by seizing complete authority, thus displacing the Jewish government and destroying the national identity. Their fears revealed a complete misunderstanding of the motives of Jesus, who had no political ambitions whatever. He had already indicated by his refusal to be made king that he had no intention of organizing a revolt against Rome.*[31]

Fear of losing their position of power led the Jewish leaders to set in motion a plan to arrest and kill Jesus. Without realizing the truth of his words, the high priest (Caiaphas) prophetically said in verse 50, "It is better for you that one man should die for the people, not that the whole nation should perish."

The High Priest is convinced that destroying Jesus would save Israel from being destroyed by Rome. He reckons that one life is cheap in contrast to the entire nation. His words have great prophetic significance. One Bible teacher notes, "Though his intent was sinful, God used him to indicate that Jesus would die for the people as a substitutionary sacrifice." And this is the irony John didn't want us to miss: Jesus' death, intended to spare the nation of Israel from physical destruction, was actually used by God to spare the world from spiritual destruction.[32]

This is the Gospel; Jesus gave His life for us so that we can have eternal life in Him. And because of Jesus, death does not have the last word. This was the basis of our hope as a family as we said goodbye to a woman we dearly loved. Our faith in Jesus, who is the Resurrection and the Life, granted us His peace that surpasses understanding. Our hope in this broken world is that death has been swallowed up in Christ's victory. As the Apostle Paul states in 1 Corinthians 15:51–57:

> *Listen, I tell you a mystery: We will not all sleep, but we will all be changed—in a flash, in the twinkling of an eye, at the last trumpet. For the trumpet will sound, the dead will be raised imperishable, and we will be changed. For the perishable must clothe itself with the imperishable, and the mortal with immortality. When the perishable has been clothed with the imperishable, and the mortal with immortality, then the saying that is written will come true: "Death has been swallowed up in victory."*
>
> *"Where, O death, is your victory?*
> *Where, O death, is your sting?"*
>
> *The sting of death is sin, and the power of sin is the law. But thanks be to God! He gives us the victory through our Lord Jesus Christ.*

Since sin entered the world in the Garden of Eden, death has reigned over humanity. Now, because of Christ, death is no longer our enemy. Take a moment to worship and pray, giving thanks to Jesus, who is your victory over sin and death!

Day 2: John 11:53–12:11

I lived for many years believing I was a Christian before *actually* becoming a disciple of Jesus. Growing up in what was once considered the Bible Belt, I knew many facts about the Lord. I could tell you where He was born, what He taught, and how and why He died. The problem was that I didn't know Jesus personally, nor had I committed my life to Him. I just knew some Bible facts. Here's the issue: a disciple not only believes the correct information concerning Jesus (i.e., He is God, offers forgiveness, and grants eternal life) but has also coupled the information with faith.

As we've seen thus far in our study, a person can know the appropriate data and still not believe in Him (i.e., the religious leaders of Jesus' day). While the facts I thought about Jesus growing up were accurate, the Bible says that even the demons know these truths and perish. A disciple is someone who has turned from sin and self-rule to follow Jesus and make Him the Lord of her life.

Today in our study, we behold two followers of Jesus who display important characteristics that should mark the lives of all disciples. First, we will see that genuine disciples are worshippers of Jesus. They adore Him, obey Him, and choose to live for His glory. The second distinction of true disciples is that others can recognize the difference Christ has made in them—there should be evidence of life change.

We see both characteristics of a genuine disciple in today's focal passage, which also marks an important division in the Gospel of John. According to some commentators, John is to be divided into four parts:

- The introduction (chapter 1)
- The book of signs (chapters 2 through 11)
- The passion narrative (chapters 12 through 20)
- The postscript (chapter 21)

Jesus declared that we should have one distinguishing mark: not political correctness or moral superiority, but love."

PHILIP YANCEY, WHAT'S SO AMAZING ABOUT GRACE?

The verses we study today are the halfway point in the Gospel and transition us to the most momentous week in world history—the passion week. This historic week began with the arrival of Jesus in Bethany on His way up to Jerusalem for the Feast of Passover where He would be crucified for the sin of the world.

Read John 11:53–57. Note the context of today's study. What threat is looming?

What is Jesus doing?

Read John 12:1–8.

John specifically notes the date of this event. When is this dinner held (verse 1)?

The host of the dinner is Simon, a man whom Jesus healed of leprosy. Also in attendance is Lazarus, whom Jesus raised from the dead. In addition to these two recipients of miracles were other eyewitnesses to these events, plus all of Jesus' disciples.

This dinner is given in Jesus' honor. What do you imagine the mood of the attendees is as they entered the party?

James Boice makes this observation about the boldness of this dinner party:

> *This supper was presumably a celebration for the raising of Lazarus. It was a brave thing for the*

WEEK 5

friends of Jesus to have done. Remember that the Sanhedrin had given an order that if anyone knew where Jesus was, they should report it to the authorities. To fail to do so would make them accessories to his crime. Still Christ's friends held this supper and held it openly.[33]

At this point, association with Jesus proved risky and required personal sacrifice. The religious leaders had a mark on His head and anyone who knew of His location was called upon to report Him. Since Bethany was only 2 miles from Jerusalem, the news of Jesus' arrival would spread quickly back to the city.

What does it tell you about these disciples and friends of Jesus that they are willing to risk their own comfort and freedom to be with Jesus?

Today as His disciple, does your relationship with Jesus require any type of personal risk or sacrifice?

Now we come to our first characteristic of a genuine disciple—worship. John tells us that the dinner party is interrupted: first by an act and then by an aroma. Mary of Bethany, the sister of Lazarus, enters the room and begins to worship Jesus.

Read John 12:3–8.
How does Mary worship Jesus?

Read the historical note about Mary's perfume in the margin. What does her worship cost her?

Mary's Perfume:
The pure nard was a fragrant oil prepared from the roots and stems of an aromatic herb from northern India. It was an expensive perfume, imported in sealed alabaster boxes or flasks which were opened only on special occasions. The cost of the oil was estimated to be a year's salary. Mary's lavish gift (a pint) expressed her love and thanks to Jesus for Himself and for His restoring Lazarus to life. The house was filled with the fragrance.[†]

[†] Blum, E. A. (1985). John. In J. F. Walvoord & R. B. Zuck (Eds.), *The Bible Knowledge Commentary: An Exposition of the Scriptures* (Vol. 2, p. 316). Wheaton, IL: Victor Books.

Worship is not merely something that occurs on a Sunday morning. It is a lifestyle of loving, adoring, and honoring Jesus. Worship is sacrificing our time and treasure to serve Him. It means living in such a way that the world sees that Jesus is supreme in our affections.

Read Romans 12:1.

What is our worship in response to?

How can you begin to live a lifestyle of worship today?

Mary models for us a lifestyle of worship, but our text also contains a marvelous statement regarding her. While her worship overflows from a heart that loves Jesus, she is also a woman who treasures His Word. John tells us that she knows that Jesus is about to suffer and die on the cross. Jesus had tried to tell the others. Hours before on the way to Jerusalem He had told the disciples:

> *We are going up to Jerusalem … and the Son of Man will be betrayed to the chief priests and teachers of the law. They will condemn him to death and will hand him over to the Gentiles, who will mock him and spit on him, flog him and kill him. Three days later he will rise.*
> *— Mark 10:33–34.*

But the disciples had not understood Him, which becomes clear in their conversation with Jesus in the Upper Room just hours before He is arrested (John 13–14). It is also evident from their hopeless reaction to His death. Only Mary understood. She had understood for some time. And she broke her box of perfume over Jesus to show Him that she understood that He was born to die as the Lamb of God.

Here's the million-dollar question. How does Mary know that Jesus is about to die just a few days from then? Time after time Jesus told His disciples that He would be arrested, crucified, and raised from the dead. Yet, when those events took place precisely as Jesus predicted, the disciples are shocked. But not Mary. Not only does she know, but she also prepares Him for His burial.

Mary knows these things because she listened.

Review these passages about Mary of Bethany in the margin. Where is Mary found and what is her posture each time she's mentioned in scripture?

> *Now as they went on their way, Jesus entered a village. And a woman named Martha welcomed him into her house. And she had a sister called Mary, who sat at the Lord's feet and listened to his teaching.*
> LUKE 10:38–39

One scholar makes this observation about Mary:

> *How did Mary understand these things when the others, particularly the disciples, failed? The answer is: by being often in the place where we find her now. Where? She is at the feet of Jesus, anointing him and wiping his feet with her hair. Where is she always? At the feet of Jesus.*[34]

> *Now when Mary came to where Jesus was and saw him, she fell at his feet, saying to him, "Lord, if you had been here, my brother would not have died."*
> JOHN 11:32

Review verses 3–8 and contrast Judas' response with Mary's adoration. What is the difference between these two?

Judas uses the smokescreen of religion to hide his true intentions. He piously talks about serving the poor, but Jesus knows what is in his heart. Judas has a weakness for money and will later betray Jesus for the sum of thirty silver coins. Judas's life had become a lie and filled with greed, and this opened the door for the devil to use him to betray Jesus.

> *Mary therefore took a pound of expensive ointment made from pure nard, and anointed the feet of Jesus and wiped his feet with her hair. The house was filled with the fragrance of the perfume.*
> JOHN 12:3

James Boice makes this striking comparison between Judas and Mary:

> *Out of his greed Judas eventually sold Christ for thirty pieces of silver, an amount probably equal to 120 denarii. Mary gave Jesus an offering worth two-and-a-half times that amount. Judas kept the bag, from which he pilfered. Mary broke her box in order that all might be given to Jesus. Judas sought to turn attention from Jesus. Mary sought to turn it to him.[35]*

Instead of hoarding for herself, Mary willingly sacrifices something sacred for Jesus. She calculates that Jesus is worth far more than her most valued possession. Her act says to the watching world, "Jesus is worthy!"

What about you? Does your life testify to the world the worth of Christ?

What are you willing to sacrifice to worship Him?

I must answer this question for myself. Our most valued possessions may be different. It may be a comfortable home, a healthy bank account, or a standard of living to which we've grown accustomed. But whatever it is, the question remains. Would we give it up for Jesus? Or is there a way that we could use it to demonstrate our love for Him?

Here's the beautiful takeaway—whatever we spend on Jesus is never wasted. Instead, it becomes a memorial that lasts for all eternity! As Jesus said, "For whoever wants to save his life will lose it, but whoever loses his life for me and for the gospel will save it" (Mark 8:35).

Now we come to the second characteristic of discipleship. Our lives should be walking testimonies of His grace, goodness, and power that lead others to follow Him.

Read John 12:9–11.
What impact does Lazarus' testimony have on people (verse 11)?

What do the religious leaders want to do to him (verse 10)?

Why do you think they want to silence Lazarus?

Lazarus caused quite a stir! People saw him (living, breathing, walking, and eating) and believed in Jesus as the Messiah! Jews were arriving in Jerusalem from all over the world for the Passover celebration. Many heard of Lazarus's resurrection, and when they learned that Jesus had returned to Bethany, they came to see them both. Lazarus is an excellent example of the power of a transformed life. While theological arguments don't convince many people, they can't deny transformation when they see it. Therefore, Jesus tells us, "Let your light so shine before men, that they may see your good works and glorify your Father in heaven" (Matthew 5:16). When the world sees Jesus, the Light of the World, alive in us, many who are captive to the darkness will turn and run to the Light!

Spend time with God in prayer. Ask the Lord to give you a heart like Mary and the ability to lead others to Jesus like Lazarus. Take time to confess anything that hinders your worship or diminishes your light.

Day 3: John 12:12-50

Messianic Prophecy: *For centuries, the Jewish people clung to promises concerning their Messiah. They believed He would be the One to set them free from oppression, conquer their enemies, and restore the throne of King David. The Old Testament is filled with precise prophecies concerning this man: where He would be born, how He would serve, and even how He would enter the city of Jerusalem.*

Historians tell us that victory parades were common in the ancient world. From Julius Caesar to Napoleon, it was expected for conquering kings to enter a city amidst cheering crowds and groans of defeated citizens. After years of war, senseless bloodshed, and finally a crushing defeat, a parade was held as the victor rode in on a horse, staking his claim. Closing my eyes, I can imagine the noise of the crowd, the stampede of horses, and children scampering over each other for just a peek as the great man entered the city. Keep this image in the forefront of your mind as we behold the next scene in the life of Christ.

For nearly two thousand years, this moment has been called Palm Sunday. Jesus' triumphal entry into Jerusalem as the King of Israel is so significant that each Gospel (Matthew, Mark, Luke, and John) makes a point to highlight the scene.

If you grew up in church, you probably participated in some type of celebration as a kid with palm leaves and a donkey colt. But to truly appreciate the significance of this event, we must understand the anticipation of the people for their King to arrive.

God is in the details. When Jesus knew that the time had come to present Himself, He was intentional that every box was checked, and every prophecy fulfilled by His entry. And when the time was right, King Jesus entered Jerusalem as the long-awaited Messiah, riding on a donkey, just as the prophets predicted He would.

Read John 12:12–19.

What event is taking place in Jerusalem that week (verse 1 and 12)?

What do the crowd wave as Jesus arrives (verse 13)?

What do they shout (verse 13)?

Read Matthew 21:1–11. (To see a different description of this Palm Sunday event.) What additional details do you learn from Matthew's account?

How does Matthew tell us that Jesus acquired the donkey colt?

Why did this specific detail take place (Matthew 21:4)?

Passover was when the Jewish people celebrated their liberation from Egyptian bondage. Jerusalem burst at the seams as visitors from across the world gathered to celebrate this sacred holiday. Many used this feast to express their longing for political freedom from Rome. They anticipated a Messiah who would defeat their oppressors, just as God did when He set them free from slavery in Egypt.

A few days before Passover, Jesus rides a donkey from the eastern side of the Mount of Olives into Jerusalem. As He enters, people spread their cloaks on the ground before Him. Then the disciples praise Him as the crowd shouts, "Hosanna," which meant, "God save us!"

This moment is rich with symbolism. For the crowd, the cry of "Hosanna" is political. They want national deliverance from the Romans. But for Jesus, this cry was the very reason He came into the world – to save us from our ultimate enemies, sin and death (John 3:16–17). So while the crowd clamors for a mighty warrior, Jesus comes as the suffering servant.

> *But when the fullness of time had come, God sent forth his Son, born of woman, born under the law, to redeem those who were under the law, so that we might receive adoption as sons. And because you are sons, God has sent the Spirit of his Son into our hearts, crying, "Abba! Father!" So you are no longer a slave, but a son, and if a son, then an heir through God.*
>
> GALATIANS 4:4–7

The people wave palm branches, a symbol that had previously been on Jewish coins when Israel was a free nation. Therefore, palm branches were not only a symbol of peace, but also political freedom. They hoped Jesus came as the Messiah who would restore Israel to her former glory.

Instead of riding in on a stallion like a Roman emperor, Jesus arrives on a donkey colt. Not only does this act fulfill prophecy, but it is a direct reference to King David, to whom God promised an eternal kingdom. When Jesus arrives on a donkey, it is a flashback to the moment, a thousand years before, when King David gave his throne to Solomon. King Solomon's coronation parade traveled down the Mount of Olives and into Jerusalem—on the very same route and on the very same animal that Jesus took. There would be no question in the mind of those who observed this event that *this was a coronation of the King of the Jews!*

Read John 12:20–26.

What does Jesus say has finally arrived in verse 23?

Throughout this Gospel we've noted how important "time" was to Jesus. Jesus understood that specific prophecies must be fulfilled. My heart races as I imagine how Jesus must have felt in that moment. Since He left His throne in glory and took on human flesh, a countdown clock had been ticking until the moment He would redeem the world. He knows the time is at hand.

Read Galatians 4:4–7 in the margin and note what you learn about Jesus' time.

While Jesus knew that His death was key to redemption, that doesn't mean that He didn't experience human agony at the thought of what He would face. The next scene shows Jesus talking to the Father about the anguish in His soul. Yes, He wants nothing more than to do His Father's will, yet He knows that His obedience will mean tremendous suffering.

Read John 12:27–36.

What is the state of Jesus' soul in verse 27? What do you think this means?

What does Jesus pray to the Father in verse 28?

What is the Father's response (verse 28)?

Concerning this heavenly exchange, Warren Wiersbe writes:

> *The prayer, "Father, glorify Thy name!" received a reply from heaven! God the Father spoke to His Son and gave Him a double assurance: the Son's past life and ministry had glorified the Father, and the Son's future suffering and death would glorify the Father.[36]*

Read John 12:37–50.

Read the entire section and note all forms of the key word "believe." How many do you find?

What does John tell us about most of the religious leaders in verse 37?

John reports that some did believe in Jesus, but secretly hid their faith. What are the reasons they denied faith in Jesus (verses 42–43)?

This temptation to deny Jesus provides a great warning to us all. Following Jesus is not always convenient or popular. The call to follow Christ can be a call for us to forsake comfort, status, and the approval of others. In some countries and cultures, the decision to follow Christ can even mean persecution or death. As followers of Jesus, we must forsake temporary human praise to gain eternal rewards.

Let's take inventory of our own hearts. When do we love the praise of man more than the praise of God? Think of times when you've been tempted to hide your faith in Christ by either your actions or your words.

Who does Jesus say He represents (verses 44–45, and 49)?

Why did Jesus come into the world (verse 47)?

What happens to someone who rejects Jesus (verse 48)?

I've sung two songs to my daughter each night since bringing her home from the hospital: "Somewhere Over the Rainbow" and "'Tis So Sweet to Trust in Jesus." Now that I think about it, these songs belong together, for they tell the story of redemption.

The first is the famous theme song from *The Wizard of Oz*. In the movie, Dorothy hopes for "somewhere over the rainbow where skies are blue" and where her "troubles melt like lemon drops." This lullaby is a longing for peace, freedom, and abundant life. In some ways, this is the same cry the crowds made when they shouted to Jesus, "Hosanna!" They desired a deliverer to save them and end their oppression. They wanted to wake up "where the clouds were far behind" them.

Don't we all!

"Hosanna" is the soul's cry for salvation.

Friends, Jesus beckons us to come to Him with childlike trust and believe that He alone fulfills this longing. As we've journeyed through this study, we've seen time and again how important the word "believe" is to this Gospel. Each of us comes to a point where we must answer, "Who is my deliverer? Will I believe in Jesus, or harden my heart and turn away from Him?"

This decision point is why I also sing "'Tis So Sweet to Trust in Jesus." I want Sydney to know that there is only One who answers our cries, fulfills our longings, and offers us peace … and His name is Jesus. I've experienced redemption, and I know firsthand that only Christ Jesus brings the peace, wholeness, and freedom for which I long. Therefore, I want my baby to drift off to sleep each night knowing, "'Tis so sweet to trust in Jesus!"

> *Tis so sweet to trust in Jesus,*
> *Just to take Him at His Word;*
> *Just to rest upon His promise,*
> *Just to know, "Thus saith the Lord!"*
>
> *Jesus, Jesus, how I trust Him!*
> *How I've proved Him o'er and o'er;*
> *Jesus, Jesus, precious Jesus!*
> *Oh, for grace to trust Him more!*

Take a moment to express your trust in Jesus. Praise Him for all the ways He has been Hosanna, the God who saves!

Day 4: John 13

When we read the word "betrayal," we feel the sting. If you've ever been betrayed by a friend or a loved one, then you know the pain that comes from another's unfaithfulness. Today in our study, we get a glimpse into the humanity of Jesus. Like us, He experienced the heartbreak of having someone He loved reject Him. But even during the betrayal, Jesus models for us extravagant love, humble service, and the posture of grace. Jesus gives us an example to follow. And from His teaching, we learn that actions do often speak louder than words.

The context of today's passage is critical. This is the Passover meal, which occurs the night before Jesus' death. He knows that His time has come, so now Jesus prepares the disciples for His impending death and departure to Heaven.

I've often heard it said that a person's final words are significant. Since Jesus knows His time is short with the disciples, He is intentional in what He conveys to them. Over the next few lessons, which lead up to the cross, we will hear Jesus impart truths, encouragement, and warnings to His followers. It is essential that we lean in close, take the posture of a devoted disciple, and listen to what He shares.

Read John 13:1–38. Try to imagine the scene, the emotions, and the conversations that took place.

What stands out to you in this story?

How would you describe the atmosphere in the room?

According to the text, how did Jesus feel about His disciples (verse 1)?

Sometimes we falsely assume God's love is based on merit. While this is the way the world works, this is not how God works. Jesus is God, and this passage reminds us that He is in full command of all that occurs. He knows who will betray, deny, and abandon Him in the upcoming hours. Yet, even with this knowledge, Jesus loves them, and demonstrates this love in a manner that is considered undignified.

I've got to be honest; this scene is medicine to my soul. I look back on my life and see countless times I have denied Christ by my actions or betrayed Him with my sin. But the comfort I take from God's Word is this: even when I feel unworthy, I am loved. Even when I've blown it, I am still a child of God. Even when I knew better, I didn't out-sin the mercy of God. His amazing grace is too wonderful to comprehend at times. But this is the message Jesus sends when He stoops down like a common servant and washes the feet of the one He knows will betray Him.

Lean in with me a little closer and hear the sloshing of water in the basin. Imagine that the One of whom the angels cry out, "Holy, Holy, Holy is the Lord God Almighty," is bending down and washing your feet. Now, hear the Lord say, "You are clean."

This is God's grace.
This is undeserved mercy.
This is Jesus.

We could stop here and just worship, but we can't miss an essential key to this story. Jesus was able to serve, love with abandon, and act with such humility because He had nothing to prove! Jesus knew exactly who He was!

According to verse 3, what does Jesus know about His identity and mission? Would you describe Jesus as confident or insecure?

How does Simon Peter react to the idea of Jesus washing his feet (verses 6–9)?

Foot Washing:
Foot washing was a common act in Biblical times. People traveled mostly on foot in sandals across the dusty roads of Judea. When entering a home, it was customary to wash one's feet. To not offer to wash a guest's feet was considered a breach of hospitality (see Luke 7:44). Washing guests' feet was a job for a household servant to carry out when guests arrived.[†]

[†] Barton, B. B. (1993). *John* (p. 272). Wheaton, IL: Tyndale House.

Jesus' response to Peter is instructive to us. The act of foot washing was symbolic of Jesus' entire ministry. He came as a servant and through His act of love (dying on the cross) we are cleansed from our sin. His response to Peter, as one scholar notes, "expresses the necessity, not only for the cleansing of Peter's feet to make him socially acceptable for the dinner, but also for the cleansing of his personality to make him fit for the kingdom of God. The external washing was intended to be a picture of spiritual cleansing from evil."[37]

After He finishes washing all their feet. What question does Jesus ask (verse 12)?

Why do you think He asked this?

What command are we given by Christ (verse 14–17)?

What promise does He give with this command (verse 17)?

Christ's actions are not only counter-cultural, but they also shocks the disciples. They still operated by the world's system, where leaders expected to be honored and served, rather than the Kingdom principle of servant leadership. Jesus emphasizes the fact that if He, their leader (Teacher and Lord), humbles Himself to serve, then they should do the same for each another.

Why is Jesus troubled in spirit (verse 21)?

Can you recall a time when you felt betrayed? What were the emotions you felt?

Do you think the others expects Judas to be the betrayer (verses 21–30)?

What does it communicate to you that Jesus still washed Judas's feet?

Who does the scripture indicate is leading and directing Judas (verses 2, 27)?

What do Jesus tell Judas to do (verse 27)?

Why did the disciples think Judas left the room (verse 29)?

Now read Luke 22:1–6 to see what Judas does when he left.

We see in the text that Simon Peter signals to his friend who occupies the place next to Jesus, asking him to find out the identity of the traitor. Simon's inquiry "demonstrated not only his persistent

> So, if you think you are standing firm, be careful that you don't fall! No temptation has overtaken you except what is common to mankind. And God is faithful; he will not let you be tempted beyond what you can bear. But when you are tempted, he will also provide a way out so that you can endure it.
>
> 1 CORINTHIANS 10:12–13

trait of curiosity but also his loyalty." Peter is a man of action and takes his place in Jesus' inner circle seriously. One could assume that he wants to step in and prevent the betrayal if he knows in advance who the person might be. Peter will become central to the storyline soon, and now we see him confident in his own loyalty, assuming the role of Jesus' defender and guardian. The irony is that he too will deny Jesus.

Read John 13:31–38.

What important command does Jesus give to His followers as He prepared them for His departure (verse 34)?

What is the result of this love (verse 35)?

What bold promise does Peter make to Jesus (verse 37)?

What does Jesus predict will happen to Peter (verse 38)?

Read 1 Corinthians 10:12–13 (In the margin).
How does this apply to Judas and Peter?

How does this truth speak to you today?

We will all be tempted to deny Christ, whether through our actions or our words. Temptations abound to choose the world rather than Jesus. But here is the promise we find in God's Word: we have the power of the Holy Spirit to resist the enemy and to stand firm in Christ. But we can't judge others when they fall; each of us is susceptible to the same temptations. We all have the same enemy who seeks to kill, steal, and destroy. Satan wants each of us to live for ourselves rather than to live for Jesus. Our responsibility is to keep our hearts devoted to Christ and to love one another.

Next week we will continue to walk verse by verse through the Gospel of John and behold God's glory in Jesus! As we come nearer to the cross, we will feel the darkness settle over Jerusalem. Next, we will observe the injustice of Christ's sacrificial death. And finally, when the sky turns pitch black over Calvary, we will hear Jesus say, "it is finished."

Take a few minutes to thank Jesus for being a God of mercy, who washes our feet and showers us with love, even when we've denied Him. Also, ask the Lord to show you someone you can serve in His name today.

Video Teaching Notes

Video teachings available for free at www.beholdandbelieve.com.

WEEK 6: BEHOLD, THE CHRIST

We have found Him of whom Moses in the Law and also the Prophets wrote—Jesus of Nazareth. — John 1:44

I. The Anointed One; Luke 4:18–21

The Hebrew word for "anoint" is important for us to understand: it is the word from which we get our English word "messiah" and refers to someone who is set apart by the LORD for special service.

> *Jesus's title, _____ means anointed one, as does its Hebrew counterpart, Messiah. When we read the Old Testament we discover three groups of people are anointed with oil to symbolize their commissioning to an office: prophets, priests, and kings. The anointing oil symbolized the Holy Spirit's outpouring upon the person for their service to the Lord.*

II. Prophet; Deuteronomy 18:15

The role of a prophet in the Old Testament was to speak the word of God. Some would foretell events, perform healings, and/or do miracles.

— *Fulfilled in Christ: John 2:19; John 6:14; John 8:28*

III. Priest

The role of a priest in the Old Testament was a mediator, or bridge, between God and human beings. He offers sacrifice to God on behalf of all. Once a year on the Day of Atonement the Jewish High Priest went into the Holy of Holies in the Temple. There he offered sacrifice to God to make up for his sins and the sins of the people.

— *Fulfilled in Christ: Hebrews 7:25–27; Hebrews 9:11–14; John 17*

IV. King; 1 Samuel 16:13, 1 Chronicles 17:11–14

As the anointed representative of the Lord, the role of the Judean king was the mediator of the covenant between the Lord and His people. They were expected to observe His covenant and laws, to defend the nation and engage in offensive war when deemed necessary, and to rule the people with justice and righteousness.

— *Fulfilled in Christ: Matthew 1:1–17; John 18:36*

V. The Son of David — The Shepherd King

The title "Son of David" is more than a statement of physical genealogy. It is a _____ title. When people referred to Jesus as the Son of David, they meant that He was the long-awaited Deliverer, the fulfillment of the Old Testament prophecies.

— *David vs. Goliath; 1 Samuel 17:32–51*

— *Jesus vs. Satan; Genesis 3:15, John 10*

SMALL GROUP QUESTIONS

1. What did you behold about Jesus in your homework this week? What did this revelation lead you to believe?
2. In today's teaching, Marian taught that a Prophet was one who spoke on behalf of God. Read John 1:14 and Hebrews 1:1–3. How did Jesus fulfill this role?
3. Why is Jesus called the Great High Priest? Read and discuss Hebrews 2:17 and 9:12–14.
4. Jesus is called the Son of David. What meaning did this title hold for the Jewish people?
5. God promised in the Garden of Eden that the "seed of the woman" would one day "crush the head" of the serpent (Genesis 3:15) How did Jesus fulfill this promise?

WEEK 6

Day 1: John 14

I love a good question. Honestly, I don't want to undersell this point; I really love to ask questions. On our first date, my husband told me that I reminded him of Barbara Walters. For those too young to know this famous journalist, she was renowned for her interviews where she probed, queried, and grilled her subjects until they were found confessing their deepest pain and crying on national television.

To be honest, Justin's assessment of me was not wrong. The poor guy sat down to his meal and didn't get to touch his food because I dove in with my barrage of questions.

That first date went something like this:
So ... tell me?
Then what happened?
How did that make you feel?
Wow, I guess you really didn't see that coming; I wonder why?

As I said, I love questions. But my inquiry paid off! By the time I happily finished my steak and began sampling his untouched French fries, I decided that I was sitting across from an incredible man. I'd be a fool if I didn't give him a chance.

Questions lead to answers. And with honest answers, the knowledge of another person grows. Relationships deepen with revelation because transparency fosters trust. So, dear reader, be warned! Should we ever sit down for coffee, prepare to be pestered. I'm not nosy (Okay, that's a lie, I am!), but mostly, I want to know you.

Today we open John 14, which is filled to the brim with questions. And I'm so thankful that it is! Because this Q&A between Jesus and His disciples reveals some of the most essential theology in the entire Bible. At the same time, it gives us some of the most practical truths for living our daily lives.

WEEK 6

Let's get started and eavesdrop on this great conversation between Jesus and the men He would use to change the world.

Read John 14.

As you read, mark every question. List each one in the space below. (Hint: Some questions are asked by the disciples, and some are asked by Jesus. List all that you see.)

To understand why Jesus is comforting the disciples, we must read these verses in context. What we read here in chapter 14 is just a continuation of the meal and conversation in chapter 13. We left our study last week with Jesus telling Peter that he would deny Him three times, which threw Peter into a tailspin. Without a doubt this possibility affected the others. If Peter could deny Jesus, what of the rest of them? Jesus also spoke of His impending departure.

Think about it, these men had left everything for the Messiah, and to learn that He would soon leave them is shattering. They are distraught. And Jesus knows that within a few short hours, they will be even more disturbed, which prompts His next statement.

Knowing this context, now write Jesus' words from verse 1.

Jesus looks beyond their temporary trouble and reassured them with a future hope. They need not be dismayed for He is leaving with a specific intention in mind. What promise does Jesus make in verses 2–3?

In this conversation, Christ reassures the bewildered disciples of His ultimate purpose. Christ uses an illustration common to people of that time, where adult sons and daughters had apartments built onto their parents' home. Jesus indicates that the reason for His departure is to make ready the place where He could welcome them home permanently. Jesus' resurrection led to His ascension to Heaven, where He prepares a home for us in the Father's house.

> How does Thomas respond to Jesus' declaration that they "know the way" (verse 5)?

> What answer does Jesus give to Thomas in verse 6?

In light of Jesus' response, James Boice gives this helpful explanation of how Jesus restores us to God's original intent:

> *Before sin entered the world, Adam and Eve enjoyed a three-fold privilege in their relation to God. First, they were in communion with God. Second, they knew God and the truth that flowed from Him. Third, they possessed spiritual life. However, they disobeyed God and fell into sin, lost this privilege. Instead of enjoying communion with God, they experienced alienation from Him. Instead of knowing truth, they fell into falsehood and error. Instead of possessing life, they began to know death. This is the human condition. We are alienated from God, ignorant of truth, and condemned to spiritual and physical death. The glory of Christ's claim is in its being a divine answer to each of these three levels. Instead of alienation, there is "the way" to God. Instead of ignorance or error, there is "the truth." Instead of death, there is "the life."*
> — J. M. Boice

We live in a pluralistic world that claims there are many paths to Heaven. There is the well-worn illustration used by philosophers to describe how man reaches God. The saying goes something like this: man is at the bottom of the mountain, and God is at the top. All religions are just different paths up the same mountain.

Perhaps you've heard this theory?

Here's the problem. This is not what Jesus said, and He is the only one who backed up His words by rising from the dead! Jesus said there is only one way, one truth, and one means to eternal life—and He is it!

What other audacious claim does Jesus make in John 14:7?

What is Philip's request in John 14:8?

How does Jesus respond in John 14:9–11?

Somewhat baffled that the disciples still didn't get it, Jesus affirms His deity, once again claiming that He and the Father are one. In verse 10, He assures them that all He taught was a direct revelation from God. He says the proof was in the ministry they witnessed for over three years.

Next, we hear Christ Jesus give vision to what will occur after His resurrection. In the following verses, Jesus describes the role of the Church in the world. (Hint: that's you and me.) Jesus tells the disciples the supernatural and world-changing work that those who believe in Him will accomplish.

What two promises does Jesus make in verses 12–14?

Jesus gives a two-fold promise. First, He guarantees that His disciples would continue His works in the world, and second He assures them that He would answer their prayers. Concerning the first promise, we see in the book of Acts that the disciples went on to do miracles, just as Jesus did. They also spread the Gospel throughout the world. So, the ministry of Jesus continues today. And you and I are part of this ongoing outpouring of God's Spirit, which is transforming lives across the globe.

We must remember, when Jesus says we can ask "for anything," that our asking must be in His name—that is, according to God's character and will. God will not grant requests contrary to His nature. We don't use His name as a magic formula to fulfill our selfish desires. If we sincerely follow Jesus and seek His will, then our requests will align with His, and He will grant them.

Considering these guarantees, who does Jesus promise to send to us (verse 16–17)?

Why do you think Jesus assures the disciples He would send them a Helper?

In these passages, Jesus begins to introduce the Holy Spirit. Little has been said about Him so far in John's Gospel. But our Helper will take center-stage in the next few chapters as Jesus prepares the disciples for life after His resurrection. Jesus wants them to know that they will not be left without the power, resources, and ability to carry out their mission.

What comfort does Jesus give in verse 18?

My mom was an orphan. At the age of two, she was abandoned on the streets by her biological parents. She carried this sting throughout her life until Jesus healed her deep wound with His indescribable love. How wonderful is it that Jesus comforts these grown men with the promise that He is not abandoning them or leaving them defenseless? He sees and knows our deepest fears. He doesn't shame us for having them, but instead, meets us in our weakness with His presence. Christ assures His disciples of His ongoing presence with them and their inclusion in the family of God.

Read John 14:19–24 and note the number of times "Love" is mentioned. Then summarize in your own words what Jesus says in this section.

In verse 26, Jesus returns to the topic of the Holy Spirit. List everything you learn about the Spirit.

What reason does Jesus give for this entire conversation (verse 29)?

Read John 14:30–31.

Jesus knows His death is imminent and tells the disciples that the "ruler of this world is coming." According to the following verses, to whom is Jesus referring (Ephesians 2:1–3, 2 Corinthians 4:4, 1 John 5:19)?

What did you learn about the "ruler of this world"?

Jesus knows the hour is at hand; it is time for Him to face the "the enemy." But because Jesus is sinless, Satan has no hold on Him. And God's ultimate will—our redemption—will be accomplished.

Let this beautiful truth give you hope in the sovereignty of our God:

> *Ironically, when Jesus died, Satan thought he had won the battle. He did not realize that Jesus' death had been part of the plan all along. In dying, Jesus' defeated Satan's power over death, for Jesus would rise again.*

Sure, Satan was the mastermind behind the death of Christ. He assumed (falsely) that killing the Messiah would bring Him victory. Yet, he had no idea that his wicked plan would backfire and through the death of Christ, God would redeem His children!

Friends, we are part of ongoing work God is doing in the world. The Church is now the presence of Jesus on earth. He gives us the Helper (Holy Spirit) to do His work. Spend a few minutes in prayer, asking Jesus for His Spirit to help you fulfill your calling in this world.

WEEK 6

Day 2: John 15:1-17

So far in John's Gospel, we've seen two distinct camps—Believers and non-believers. Both witnessed the miracles, heard His teachings, and were confronted with the same question: What do we do with the claims of Jesus Christ? These claims center around the "I Am" statements of Christ, which are a revelation of His divinity and an invitation to experience life in Him.

Today, we read the seventh "I Am" statement. Jesus shares this message privately with His disciples as He prepares them for life after His departure. Jesus illustrates what a relationship with Him looks like and what this divine connection produces. In these verses we discover the key to an abundant life.

Our study of John 14 concluded with a transition as Jesus said, "Rise, let us go from here." At that point, they left the Upper Room, where they ate the Passover meal and began walking to the Garden of Gethsemane. The teaching found in John 15 occurs somewhere along this journey.

Imagine a full Passover moon brightening the sky as they walk by torchlight along the cobbled Jerusalem streets. Many scholars believe Jesus pauses in front of the Temple, the symbol of the Jewish faith, and shares this important lesson. The Temple was quite a sight to behold. Adorned with gold, it had an intricate vine emblazoned on the front. The vine was the national emblem of Israel. There, in front of the symbol of their faith, Jesus says "I Am the true vine."

Read John 15:1–11.

How many times is the word "abide" or "remain" used?

Based upon this initial reading, what is your understanding of this word?

Who does Jesus identify as the Vine (verses 1 and 5)?

Who are the branches?

Who is the Gardener or Vinedresser?

Why does He choose this symbol to describe Himself? A vine is a stem that connects to the roots in the ground so that branches can pull nutrients from it. Likewise, Jesus is the Vine that is rooted in heaven so that we can connect to the life of God. Pastor Tim Keller makes this observation:

> *Through Christ, the Vine, whose roots are in the Godhead, we can enter into the life of God. God's life interpenetrates our lives, and the result (as when the life of the stem interpenetrates the life of the branch) of us coming into the nature of God through Christ is supernaturally fueled character change."*[38]

When we are united with Christ, then we draw life, energy, and resources directly from His divine power. To be a branch in the Vine means we are united to Christ and participate in His life. As we abide in Him, His life flows through us and produces fruit.[39]

Read the following passages and make note of what you discover about your union with Christ:
Galatians 2:20, 2 Peter 1:3–4, Romans 8:9–11

Christianity is not simply a set of beliefs or rules to follow. Faith in the Risen Christ makes us new creations. Pastor Tim Keller explains:

> "Being born again means your heart has been uprooted and replanted into a new stem and into new soil. The very life of heaven has come into your life. Union with Christ is the basis for our growth."[40]

In this beautiful relationship between us (the branches) and Christ (the Vine), God the Father is the Gardener (or Vinedresser). To achieve their best productivity, grapevines require care and attention. Now let's see God the Father's role in our spiritual growth:

According to John 15:2, what are two things the Vinedresser (Gardener) does to the branches?

In Verse 2 Jesus says, "Every branch in me that does not bear fruit he takes away." The phrase "takes away" can confuse many. In the original language, it is better understood to say the Vinedresser "lifts up" the branch.

Perhaps your image of vineyards is lush trellises in France or California. Unfortunately, these are not the picture of grapevines in ancient Israel, where vines grew along the ground, close to the soil. As a result, when the rains would fall, some branches would get buried under the mud. Therefore, a caring gardener would "lift up" or "take away" the branch from the muck and clean it off. The vinedresser does this so that the branch can produce fruit.

We, too, get trampled in the mud and require cleansing. This is a picture of sin in our lives. Because God loves us, He convicts us of the sin, invites us to repent, and lifts us out of the mess. God cleanses and restores us so that our lives can bear fruit.

This care of God is beautifully described in Psalm 40 (see Margin). I love this image of our God. He is for us, not against us. His tender care for us is so that we can have the most abundant lives imaginable.

> *I waited patiently for the Lord; he turned to me and heard my cry.*
> *He lifted me out of the slimy pit, out of the mud and mire; he set my feet on a rock and gave me a firm place to stand.*
>
> PSALM 40:1–2

Verse 2 also describes how the Vinedresser (The Father) "prunes" fruitful branches. Ouch! While we don't like this idea, it proves to be a blessing. We see this spiritual truth played out in nature all around us. Each winter, we cut back the shrubs around our house so that they will bloom in the spring. During February, those branches look haggard, but by the time May rolls around, the lush flowers and happy bees tell us that the pruning was worth it!

When God removes something or someone from our lives, it may not feel pleasant, but long-term blessings come from those cuts. Pruning has taken different forms in my life—a closed door, a setback, an ending of a relationship, an illness, or a heartbreak. My most profound season of pruning was what God used to propel me into full-time ministry. While the two years of pruning hurt like the dickens, I would not be the woman I am today if God had left me unpruned.

Pruning: *The removal of dead stems and cutting branches back, closer to the vine.*

What's the purpose of pruning? To get a branch to draw nutrients from the vine in a way it never has before. The same is true for us; when we get "cut back," we draw closer to Jesus. Anything that causes us to rely more on Christ will only result in more fruit in our lives.

Have you ever experienced a pruning season? What event or circumstances caused you to draw closer to Jesus?

Looking back at the text (John 15:1–17), what did Jesus say was the key is to a fruitful life? (Hint: this word is repeated almost 10 times.)

Consider the vine-branch relationship. Can a branch produce grapes if cut off from the vine? Why or why not (verses 4–5)?

According to Jesus, what are you able to do apart from Him?

Now that we recognize our utter dependence on Christ, what does it mean to "abide" or "remain" in the vine? This word means to depend or rely upon. Just as the branch depends on the vine for nutrients, so we're supposed to depend on Jesus for spiritual life. We stay connected to Him through reading His word and prayer, we remain rooted in His love, and we rely on His power through the Holy Spirit.

There is a marked difference in my attitude and my response to circumstances when I begin my day in God's Word and prayer. Abiding in Christ empowers me with the strength I need to face the challenges of each day. When I abide, I see the fruit of the Spirit, and when I do not, unfortunately I see the rotten fruit of my flesh.

What spiritual fruit is produced in us when we abide according to Galatians 5:22–23 (see margin)?

What then is the result of our abiding (John 15:8)?

What does Jesus call us to abide "in" specifically (verse 9)?

As the vine draws nutrients from the ground that give life to the branches, so Christ draws life from the Godhead that is then poured into us. The overflow of the life of one connected to Jesus is God's love, joy, peace, kindness and gentleness blessing others.

> "Do not waste time bothering whether you 'love' your neighbor; act as if you did. As soon as we do this we find one of the great secrets. When you are behaving as if you loved someone, you will presently come to love him."
>
> C. S. LEWIS,
> MERE CHRISTIANITY

What reason does Jesus give for these instructions (verse 11)?

Happiness fluctuates like the stock market. Joy, however, is consistent. Genuine joy can't be stolen by a thief, hindered by a setback, or tackled by a linebacker. Joy is our baseline when our connection with Jesus is secure, when we draw upon His love, and when we walk in obedience to His truth. Friend, I've discovered the hard way that if my life lacks joy, then my life lacks Jesus. That's all there is to it. Jesus equals joy.

Finally, read John 15:12–17.

What command does Jesus give us in verse 12?

What does Jesus call His disciples to do in verse 14?

What is Christ's final command in verse 17?

Three simple words: "Love each other." Here's what I appreciate about Jesus: more than merely commanding us to love others, He also empowers us to do it. The very first fruit of the Holy Spirit is love. As we remain connected to Christ, His life fills us and flows through us. He called His disciples to love because He knew the world they'd be sent to would be hostile and they would desperately need each other. And it's still true today; we need each other!

What have you been attempting to do in your own strength, apart from Christ? Take some time to talk to Jesus about your inability and commit yourself to a deeper dependence on Him.

Day 3: John 15:18-16:33

My four-year old daughter Sydney has entered a new stage, which we've coined the "planning phase." The girl's got plans and wants to be prepared for all scenarios. From the moment she awakens, she wants to know, in precise detail, what events are on her schedule. Since she only goes to "school" two days a week, she has ample time to plan social activities and bombards me with places she can go and people she can see when she's not otherwise occupied.

For instance, if it is a Thursday morning, she begins the day by asking: "Where am I going today?" After I give her an overview, she then proceeds to ask, "Can I invite my friends over?" However, she doesn't stop with the current day; she then wants a detailed explanation of what to expect throughout the weekend, including her wardrobe choices and whom she might encounter.

She's only four, and I'm not able to keep up with her social calendar. But I'm learning to embrace it: planning is my daughter's superpower. One day she will greatly appreciate the moment we study today in Jesus' life. In this passage, we hear Him prepare the disciples with specific details for what will occur after His departure.

This section of John's Gospel takes place the night before Jesus was crucified. These are His final hours before His arrest. In the passage, Jesus prepares the disciples for three things:

- He prepares them for the world's hatred that will result in persecution.
- He prepares them for the personal indwelling of the Holy Spirit, who is coming to be their Helper, Counselor, and Teacher.
- He prepares them for the joy they will experience at His resurrection.

Sydney will be thrilled when she's old enough to read this section. So much preparation! Truthfully, I'd be lying if I didn't say my child gets her "need to know" honest. My best friends can tell you that information is my love language. I don't want to be caught off guard

> **World:**
> When Jesus speaks of "the world" in this passage, He is not referring to the earth or to humans. He is speaking of a world-system or cosmos that is opposed to God and hates truth and righteousness. This world-system is characterized throughout the Bible as the domain of darkness and it is under the control of the evil one, whom Jesus says is the "father of lies." Headed by Satan, this system is built on love of self, greed, and pride. Therefore, it operates in lies instead of truth, darkness instead of light, and selfishness instead of God's sacrificial love.

by bad news or the last one to know I have lipstick on my teeth. My love for information is one of the reasons this passage gives me such comfort—Jesus intentionally equips us for life in a hostile world.

Read John 15:18–16:4.

What does Jesus tell the disciples to expect (John 15:18)?

Why does Jesus say "the world" hates Christ-followers (verses 18–25)?

Read the Word Study "World" in the margin.

How have you seen this world-system at work in our culture today?

Warren Wiersbe offers this clear warning:

> The world system functions on the basis of conformity. As long as a person follows the fads and fashions and accepts the values of the world, he or she will "get along." But the Christian refuses to be "conformed to this world" (Romans 12:2) … and no longer wants to live the "old life" (1 Peter 4:1–4). We are the light of the world and the salt of the earth (Matt. 5:13–16), but a dark world does not want light and a decaying world does not want salt! In other words, the believer is not just "out of step"; he is out of place!) [41]

According to Romans 12:2, how are we supposed to relate to the world?

Why does Jesus warn us about persecution and the world's hatred (John 16:1–4)?

> *Do not be conformed to this world, but be transformed by the renewal of your mind, that by testing you may discern what is the will of God, what is good and acceptable and perfect.*
>
> ROMANS 12:2

Jesus told us in advance so that when we are harshly criticized, snubbed, or outright rejected, we can take heart knowing that just as the world hates us, it first hated Jesus.

Now Jesus turns the conversation to a much more pleasant topic—the gift of the Holy Spirit. In context, we can see why the disciples needed this subject addressed. Jesus has warned that an hour is coming when they will be persecuted, and this prospect has troubled their hearts.

Addressing the elephant in the room, Jesus reminds them that He is not abandoning them. Obviously, the disciples fear being left alone, without their leader, in a hostile world. Therefore, Jesus circles back to the promise He made earlier concerning the Holy Spirit.

Read John 16:4–14.

What is the emotional state of the disciples at this news (John 16:6)?

Write John 16:7.

The word "advantage" means a superiority of position or condition. Now let's stop and absorb this truth. Jesus tells the fellas, "It is far better ... it is superior ... it's to your advantage that I go away." Now, that is a hard pill to swallow. These men had lived with Jesus for over three years. They experienced His divine power, they witnessed His supernatural healings, they beheld His glory, and they were beneficiaries of His unconditional love. And Jesus has the nerve to say that life without Him physically present would be better?

Whom did Jesus promise to send to them (John 16:7–8)?

List everything you learn about the Holy Spirit in the following passages:

John 15:26–27, John 16:8–11, John 16:13–15

What specific names does Jesus give to the Spirit? And what pronouns does Jesus use in referring to the Spirit?

Whom does the Holy Spirit bear witness of and testify about (John 15:26)?

Whom does the Holy Spirit seek to glorify? (John 16:14)

The Holy Spirit exists to shine a spotlight on Jesus. I guess you could say that's His mission statement. He wants people to know and love the Son of God. He's involved in every aspect of our relationship with Jesus. The Spirit is the One who first convicts us of our sin so we can see our need for a Savior. Then He opens our hearts to believe the Gospel. Then, after we are born again (regenerated by the Spirit), He comes to live with us. His indwelling presence is how we live out the Christian life.

The Spirit desires more than anything else to glorify and exalt Jesus Christ. He illuminates the Bible, so we can know Jesus. He empowers us to produce Christ-like character and imparts spiritual gifts to us to further the Kingdom of God across the globe.

Now we turn our attention to the final piece of information Jesus shares with the disciples to prepare them for His departure.

Read John 16:16–33.

Why are the disciples confused and perplexed (verses 16–19)?

Since Jesus is God, He knows all things before they happen. He understands that His death is imminent, but He also knows that He will rise again. But the disciples do not yet grasp all that is going to occur. They are puzzled over the language Jesus uses. So, He gives them an illustration to help them understand.

What promise does Jesus give them in verse 20?

What analogy does Jesus give to illustrate the emotional roller-coaster that will soon happen (verse 21)?

The Holy Spirit:
The Bible reveals that God is Triune: Father, Son, and Holy Spirit. Each person of the trinity is fully God. The Spirit is a Person—not a force or phantom. Jesus referred to the Spirit as "He" and not "it." The Holy Spirit has a mind (Rom. 8:27), a will (1 Cor. 12:11), and emotions (Gal. 5:22–23). Jesus also said the Spirit is equal with God (John 15:26). So let's keep this in mind: the One who indwells a believer is a real person, with thoughts, feelings, and desires, who also just happens to be the third person of the Trinity. That's why we call Him the "Holy" Spirit.

What emotion will the disciples experience after the resurrection (verse 22)?

Why does God the Father love us (verse 27)?

What does Jesus declare about Himself (verse 28)?

How do the disciples respond to this declaration (verses 29–30)?

What reassurance does Jesus give in verse 33?

"Peace" is an interesting word choice. This is not the emotion we see on the disciples, but we do see it on Jesus. He is prepared to face His destiny. He is not anxious. He is in command and carefully instructs His disciples. Jesus' life is not measured by months or weeks anymore, but by hours. And He chooses to spend the last ones on earth with His own.

Alone with His friends, He explains how they can experience an unhindered connection with Him through the Spirit and promises them His peace in a hostile world. But He also promises one more thing—joy! While it probably seems unbelievable to them in the moment, soon these eleven men will come to understand the prophetic meaning of King David's words:

*Weeping may last through the night,
but joy comes with the morning.*
— Psalm 30:5

Conclude your study of God's Word today by talking to the Lord about what you've learned and invite Him to grow your awareness of His presence in and with you.

Day 4: John 17

I came to know Jesus as my Savior at Second Baptist Church in Houston, Texas. This is one of those massive mega-churches that people love to criticize. I'm not one of those people. For it was there that I first truly heard the Gospel and fell in love with Jesus. That church became a hospital for my weary soul, and God surrounded me with incredible people who taught me truth and showered me with Christ's love. One of my favorite things about this church is something that happens every Sunday morning.

At the conclusion of the worship service, when the TV cameras turn off, the massive black-out blinds covering the stained-glass windows are rolled up. As the blinds lift, the blazing sun breaks through and illuminates the whole room. The sunlight streams through two immense stained-glass windows that bank the front of the sanctuary. On the left is the creation window, which depicts the Garden of Eden. On the right is the Heaven window, which depicts worshippers surrounding the throne of God.

As the windows are revealed the choir sings:

*This is holy ground
We're standing on holy ground
For the Lord is here
And where He is, is holy* [42]

I'm about to cry, just thinking about the beauty and symbolism of this moment. Between the two stain-glassed gardens stand the redeemed of the Lord, lifting their voices in praise to a Holy God. Indeed, it is holy ground.

The text we read today is also holy ground. We behold Jesus, the Son of God, also standing between two gardens—as the Mediator between Heaven and Earth. He lifts His eyes to Heaven and prays to His Father. Someone once termed this chapter "the Holy of Holies of John's Gospel." Today we get a front row seat as the blinds are pulled back and we behold the love that has existed for all eternity between Father and Son.

Read John 17.

What request does Jesus make of the Father (verse 1)?

How does Jesus define eternal life (verse 3)?

Just as the Father gave authority to the Son, so the Son in turn gives eternal life to those who believe in Him. How cool is that? Jesus defines eternal life as having a personal knowledge of the living God. How is this life experienced? One of my favorite theologians offers an explanation:

Our first step toward eternal life includes realizing we don't have it. That sense of separation, rebellion, lostness, or inadequacy before God is defined as "sin" in the Bible. When we admit our sin, turn away from it and then to Christ, Christ's love lives in us through the Holy Spirit. Eternal life is not just being around forever; for believers it means eternity with God, their loving Father.[43]

According to verse 4, how did Jesus glorify the Father? (See Word Study: "Glorify" in margin to fully answer this question.)

What does Jesus reveal about His eternal existence in verse 5?

Marvel with me that the One who utters this prayer is the same One who spoke solar systems into orbit. He is the same God who upholds the universe. Mind-boggling! In this prayer, Jesus pulls back the veil to give us a glimpse of His relationship with the Father that has existed since before the dawn of time. And soon, after He is resurrected, Jesus will return to His exalted position at the right hand of God.

Read Philippians 2:5–11 and answer the following:

What do you learn about Jesus from this passage?

Where is Christ now (verse 9)?

When we confess Jesus as Lord, who is glorified (verse 11)?

Glorify:

Our English word "glory" is translated from the Greek word doxa, which indicates the high opinion of a person by others. In the New Testament this word emphasizes the majesty of God seen in His self-revelation. When Christ speaks of His actions bringing God glory, He means that the beauty and majesty of God's nature has been revealed in what He has done.[†]

[†] Richards, L. O. (1991). *The Bible reader's companion* (electronic ed., p. 694). Wheaton: Victor Books.

How is this a direct answer to what Christ prayed in John 17:1–5?

Read John 17:6–19.

In these verses the focus of Christ's prayer shifts. Who does Jesus pray for now (verses 6–8)?

List a few things that He asks the Father to do for His disciples (verses 9–19).

In this sacred moment, Jesus turns His attention to intercede for the disciples. Obviously, our Lord wants them to hear His petitions. In some ways, the prayer takes the form of a progress report on the success of Jesus' ministry.

What does Jesus specifically ask the Father to do for the disciples in verse 15?

What does Jesus pray for us in verse 17?

The word "sanctify" means to be set apart unto God for His service. Salvation is a one-time event that occurs the moment someone places faith in Jesus. Sanctification, however, is a life-long process of becoming more like Jesus in our actions, attitudes, and affections. Therefore, Jesus prays for us to be sanctified by the truth.

How does this work? As we behold the truth of who God is in the Bible, revelation causes transformation. As Jesus is revealed to our hearts, we grow to love Him and long to follow His commands. And as we do, we in turn, become more like Him. This life-long journey of knowing, loving, and following Christ is sanctification. This is the supernatural work that Jesus prayed would take place in our lives.

If you've personally trusted in Jesus as your Savior, how have you been sanctified over the past year or 10 years? How are you different today than you were before?

Write John 17:18.

According to Matthew 5:14–16 (in margin) what does Jesus say a disciple's relationship should be to the world?

> *You are the light of the world. A city set on a hill cannot be hidden. Nor do people light a lamp and put it under a basket, but on a stand, and it gives light to all in the house. In the same way, let your light shine before others, so that they may see your good works and give glory to your Father who is in heaven.*
>
> MATTHEW 5:14–16

Concerning our call to be the light of the world, one Bible commentary writes:

> *Jesus came into the world on a mission for the Father; so he sent these disciples into the world on a mission by the Son. That mission was to make God known. This is an important and exciting theme in John's Gospel. The Father sent the Son into the world, the Father and the Son send the Spirit to the disciples, and the disciples are sent by the Father and Son into the world.*[44]

Now we come to a moment in scripture that just gives me chills. We get the privilege of hearing what Jesus prayed for us. How amazing is that? Jesus prays for those who would come to believe in Him because of His disciple's ministry. And if you are a follower of Christ today, that is you!

Read John 17:20–26.

What does Jesus pray for us in verse 21?

According to verse 23, what is the result of our unity or oneness? (Hint look for what follows the words "so that.")

What is Jesus' desire for us (verse 24)?

Finally, what does Jesus pray to be "in" us (verse 26)?

Of the myriad of things that Jesus could have asked for, He asks for the Father to love us just as the Father loves Him. He wants us immersed in the deep river of love that has flowed eternally between the Father, Son, and the Spirit. As we are united with Christ, our lives overflow with the Spirit and then God's love spills forth. This love is what we were created for and the river of life for which our souls thirst. Let this truth sink deep into your heart: as Jesus faced His final hours, He prayed for you to experience the depths of His Father's love.

Today, on this sacred ground, we heard our Redeemer pray for Himself, His disciples, and for the Church. The theme of glory runs through this prayer from beginning to end and reminds us why Jesus came, why He died, and why He rose from the grave!

> "Grace teaches us that God loves because of who God is, not because of who we are."
>
> PHILIP YANCEY, WHAT'S SO AMAZING ABOUT GRACE?

This prayer encompasses the entirety of Christ's mission and ministry:

- He came from heaven to earth to reveal the Father and show the way back into His presence.
- As He declared God's word to the disciples, they believed, and the great work of redeeming humanity began.
- Jesus prayed for His followers, the Church, to be transformed by the truth and protected from the evil one so that they could spread the Gospel across the globe.

Friend, if you are holding a Bible in your hands today, you are living proof that Jesus' prayer was answered! The Holy Spirit worked through the apostles to record their eyewitness accounts of Jesus, recalling His teachings, and giving instructions to the newly formed Church.

Close your time in God's Word by tuning your heart to receive the love of God. Sit in His presence and allow His Spirit to flood your being with the reality that you are God's beloved.

Video Teaching Notes

Video teachings available for free at www.beholdandbelieve.com.

WEEK 7: BEHOLD, THE REDEEMER

> *Later, knowing that everything had now been finished, and so that Scripture would be fulfilled, Jesus said, … "It is finished." With that, he bowed his head and gave up his spirit.* — John 19:28–30

I. The Feast of Passover; Leviticus 23:4–14; Exodus 12:1–14, 43–48

- The Feast of Passover celebrated the Israelites' _____ from 400 years of slavery in Egypt.
- The final plague was the death of the _____ of every family, as the angel of death would _____ over Egypt.
- Salvation came from the blood of a _____ lamb.
- On the 10th day of the month, a lamb was taken into the home and observed for _____ days to guarantee perfection.
- At 3 p.m. on the 5th day (the 14th of Nissan), the father of each home would bring the spotless _____ to the doorstep, and slay it.
- The _____ was then applied to the doorpost of the home.
- Under the blood covering, they were _____ from the plague. They had _____ that God would save them because He could see it.
- As the angel of death passed over Egypt, he sought entrance into every household. If the home was _____, the angel of death did not enter, but instead "passed over" that house. Those under the covering of blood were given _____.

II. Jesus, Our Passover Lamb; Luke 22:14-16 and Matthew 26:26–28)

> *Behold, the Lamb of God, who takes away the sin of the world!* — John 1:29

- The Hebrew people celebrated Passover each year in Jerusalem. Jesus deliberately arranged His itinerary around the _____, testing, and _____ of the Passover lamb.

- _____ days prior to Passover, Jesus entered Jerusalem on Palm Sunday. On this exact day, the Hebrew people chose their _____ and set them aside for inspection. (John 12:12–13)
- Although they tried to trick and discredit him, _____ was found in Him. (John 19:4)
- Five days after Jesus entered Jerusalem, He was sentenced to _____ by crucifixion.
- At 9 a.m. as the _____ were prepared for sacrifice at the Temple, Jesus was _____ to the cross. (Mark 15:25) At noon the sky turned _____.
- Jesus' last words were: _____. (John 19:28–30)
- At 3 p.m. Jesus _____. (Mark 15:33–37)

> For you know that it was not with perishable things such as silver or gold that you were redeemed from the empty way of life handed down to you from your ancestors, but with the precious blood of Christ, a lamb without blemish or defect. He was chosen before the creation of the world but was revealed in these last times for your sake. — Peter 1:18–20

SMALL GROUP QUESTIONS

1. What did you behold about Jesus in your homework this week? What did this lead you to believe?
2. How did Jesus' life and death fulfill the Feast of Passover?
3. At the first Passover, the Hebrew people were set free from physical slavery. According to Jesus in John 8:34–36, what are we enslaved to? Who sets us free?
4. What do the following scriptures declare about the human state apart from faith in Jesus Christ? Romans 3:23, Romans 6:23, Ephesians 2:1–3
5. What is true of those who are "covered by the blood of the Lamb" according to Matthew 26:26–28; Romans 5:8–10; Ephesians 2:11–14; and 1 Peter 1:18–20?
6. Marian said, "Something is worth what someone is willing to pay for it." How do you feel knowing God paid the highest possible price to redeem you?

WEEK 7

Day 1: John 18:1-28

Today's focal passage is one of my favorites. I love how it brings the redemption story full circle from the Garden of Eden to the Garden of Gethsemane. The entire Bible tells of God's love and intention to restore us to His presence. Now we see the Son of God step forward, in a garden, to fulfill the purpose for which He was born.

Warren Wiersbe makes this marvelous connection:

> *Human history began in a Garden and the first sin of man was committed in that Garden. The first Adam disobeyed God and was cast out of the Garden, but the Last Adam was obedient as He went into the Garden of Gethsemane (1 Corinthians 15:45). In a Garden, the first Adam brought sin and death to mankind; but Jesus, by His obedience, brought righteousness and life to all who will trust Him.[45]*

It is no wonder that as we enter the Garden of Gethsemane, the scene of Jesus' arrest, we see Christ in full command. He is fulfilling His role as the Messiah. He knows His identity as the Lamb of God and will not bypass the sufferings of the cross. Yes, He suffered cruelly, but it was Jesus' decision to lay down His life. Don't let anyone ever tell you otherwise.

It cheapens God's grace if we don't see redemption for what it is—Jesus intentionally placing Himself on the cross instead of you and me. Substitutionary atonement is the big theological term for this act—where the death of a substitute covers the sin of another. In the passage we study today, Jesus steps forward as that substitute and offers Himself for you and me.

Read John 18:1–11.

WEEK 7

Describe this scene (verses 1–3).

How does Judas know of this specific location (verse 2)?

Judas brings a detachment of soldiers to arrest Jesus. Who else is with them and what do you recall about this group (verse 3)? (Hint: This is the religious leadership.)

These men are experts in the Old Testament and have heard Jesus' teachings and witnessed His miracles. Of all people, they should know that Jesus perfectly fulfilled the prophecies about the Messiah. But they reject Him, threaten the people not to follow Him, and orchestrate His arrest and crucifixion.

According to verse 4, who is really in command?

What name do the soldiers give for the one they are seeking (verse 5)?

How does Jesus respond (verse 5)?

What occurs to Judas and the soldiers after Jesus says "I am" (verse 6)?

Historians tell us that a Roman cohort could have numbered as many as 600 soldiers. But they, along with the religious leaders, all fall backward when Jesus answers, "I am He." Apparently, Jesus' reply is accompanied by a momentary flash of His glory. For fully armed soldiers to fall to the ground in the presence of this unarmed man shows this is not merely "Jesus the Nazarene." This is God in human flesh!

What does Jesus do next that evokes images of the Good Shepherd (verses 8–9)?

Next, Peter takes out his sword in an attempt to defend Jesus (verse 10). Do you think Peter understands yet that Jesus must die?

Sure, Peter is loyal. But unfortunately, Peter's actions stem from misunderstanding God's purpose for the cross. He is still trying to prevent Jesus' death. (See Matthew 16:21–23.)

What is Jesus' response to Peter's actions (verse 11)?

Ponder this significant moment. It was in a garden that the first Adam succumbed to Satan's snare, and sin entered the world (Genesis 3). Now here, in another garden, Jesus, the second Adam, triumphs over Satan (who controlled Judas). Even though He could have evaded arrest, Jesus deliberately goes to the place where Judas knows to find Him. As we've seen, Jesus knows all things that are coming and boldly steps out of the darkness to ask, "Whom do you seek?"

Jesus' reply, "I am," was what He used to affirm His deity in John 8:58. Although the soldiers don't get it, John, who penned this eyewitness account, doesn't want us to miss it. Jesus is the Lord God Almighty, Creator of Heaven and Earth!

After John details for us Jesus' arrest in the garden, he gives us an eyewitness account of Jesus' trial and Peter's denial. These two critical events are played out side-by-side. Before reading about Jesus' trials by the Jewish rulers, read the historical background in the margin.

Read John 18:12–18.

Where is Jesus taken after they leave the garden (verse 13)?

Where is Peter permitted to enter (verse 15)?

What are the circumstances of Peter's first denial (verse 16–17)?

According to verse 18, what is Peter standing near and what is he doing? (Tuck this little nugget of information away for later.)

Read John 18:19–24.

What does Annas, the High Priest, pressure Jesus to tell him?

What is Jesus' defense? (Verse 20)

Jesus on Trial:

Jesus faced two trials: one before the Jewish ruling council and the other before the Roman civil authorities. The Jewish leaders did not possess the power to sentence Jesus to death; they required the Roman authorities to do that. The Sanhedrin was the Jewish ruling council, which was led by the High Priest. Two names are given for the High Priest. The first is Annas, the elder, who was removed from office by Rome. The younger is Caiaphas, who is legally the High Priest but is still under the thumb of Annas. Both men interrogate Jesus.

> The Lord turned and looked straight at Peter. Then Peter remembered the word the Lord had spoken to him: "Before the rooster crows today, you will disown me three times." And he went outside and wept bitterly.
>
> LUKE 22:61–62

Jesus' first Jewish trial before Annas is like a hearing. Annas is searching for evidence with which to accuse Jesus that would lead to capital punishment. He wants to know about His teachings, disciples, and intentions. Jesus reminds him that nothing was said or done in secret; all that He did was in public. At this, one of the soldiers strikes Jesus across the face. Meanwhile, Peter is standing in the courtyard just outside of Annas's home, warming himself by a charcoal fire. John returns the story to this courtyard for us to see Peter's second and third denial of Christ.

Read John 18:25–27.

As a reminder, what did Jesus tell Peter in John 13:38?

According to Luke 22:61–62 (in the margin) what happens as Peter utters his final denial? How do you think Peter feels the moment Jesus' prophecy of his denial comes true?

At the conclusion of Jesus' interrogation by Annas, where is he sent (verse 24)?

Jesus is transferred from the Jewish trial to a Roman one before dawn. We know this because of the timing of Peter's denial. One scholar makes this important note, "The same rooster that announced the third denial of Peter also welcomed the day that Jesus was to be crucified."[46]

In our study today, we saw Jesus fully in command. However, that doesn't mean the rejections He faced didn't affect Him. First, Judas led the mob to arrest Him and then one of His closest disciples, Peter, denied Him. I imagine it crushed Jesus as much as it did Peter to watch His dear friend deny even knowing Him.

Mark's Gospel tells us that in the Garden of Gethsemane, Jesus told Peter to "Watch and pray that you may not enter into temptation. The spirit indeed is willing, but the flesh is weak" (Mark 14:38). We know Peter was not able to stand against this temptation. His flesh was weak, but even in the face of denial, Jesus loved him.

Have you ever blown it like Peter? Can you relate to the failure and shame that Peter must have felt?

Peter represents all of us, and as Jesus faced the cross, it was for all our failures that He prepared to die. Peter's failure reminds me of the hymn, "Jesus Paid it All." Read these lyrics (or listen to the song on YouTube) and allow God's grace to pour over your heart.

> *I hear the Savior say,*
> *"Thy strength indeed is small,*
> *Child of weakness, watch and pray,*
> *Find in Me thine all in all."*
>
> *Jesus paid it all, All to Him I owe;*
> *Sin had left a crimson stain,*
> *He washed it white as snow.*
>
> *Lord, now indeed I find*
> *Thy pow'r and Thine alone,*
> *Can change the leper's spots*
> *And melt the heart of stone.*
>
> *For nothing good have I*
> *Where-by Thy grace to claim;*
> *I'll wash my garments white*
> *In the blood of Calvary's Lamb.*
>
> *And when, before the throne,*
> *I stand in Him complete,*
> *"Jesus died my soul to save,"*
> *My lips shall still repeat.*[47]
> — "Jesus Paid It All," Elvina Hall

Each one of us, like Peter, carries shame that can only be cleansed by the blood of the Lamb. As you conclude your time in God's Word today, imagine yourself standing before the throne of God, forgiven, covered in white garments, and ransomed by the blood of Christ. Express your praise to Jesus in prayer.

Day 2: John 18:28-40

Since the opening chapter of John, we've seen Jesus described as the "Lamb of God who takes away the sin of the world" (John 1:29). This truth was first proclaimed by John the Baptist, and then validated time and again by Jesus, who said He came to lay down His life.

Jesus' death on the cross satisfied the requirement of the Old Testament sacrificial system to make atonement for sin. In addition, Christ stands as the fulfillment of the Passover lamb. Since we've already studied the Feast of Passover, I won't repeat those details. However, I do want to make one important note that pertains to today's text.

During the Feast of Passover, each Jewish family picked a lamb for sacrifice. But first, they brought the chosen lamb into their homes, where it would live for four days for a thorough inspection. This evaluation time was to determine if the lamb was "without blemish"(Exodus 12:5).

Only a spotless, perfect lamb could serve as the Passover lamb. I submit to you that Jesus endured this same inspection. Since the moment He entered Jerusalem on Palm Sunday, He was under the microscope. The other Gospels share in detail how the religious leadership pestered Him with questions and tried to trap Him in sin.

Yet, every step of the way, Jesus passed the test and walked in obedience to God the Father.

Today we come to the final scrutiny of the Lamb of God. After Jesus' arrest, He is interrogated by the Jewish leadership, who have no authority to put Him to death. For this reason, they send Him to Pilate, who begins his own examination of Jesus, which he concludes by saying, "I find no fault in this man" (Luke 23:4, John 19:4). John includes this to show that our Savior was indeed tried and found "not guilty." He is the spotless, perfect, and chosen Lamb of God who takes away our sin.

Read John 18:28–40.

Recall that Jesus was interrogated all night by the Jewish leaders, and He witnessed Peter's final betrayal as the rooster welcomed the dawn. What do you imagine is Jesus' physical state as He is led to see Caiaphas (verse 28)?

Why do the religious leaders not enter Caiaphas's headquarters (verse 28)?

Pilate's palace was called the Praetorium. It is here that Jesus is brought in the early morning hours after His Jewish trial. The leaders must have been desperate to get rid of Jesus, for typically, the Jews would never turn over an Israelite to the despised Romans. It is speculated that Pilate already knew about their charges against Jesus, because he is the one who instructed the Roman soldiers to arrest Him.

But still, the leaders refuse to even enter Pilate's home. One commentary gives this explanation:

> *Afraid of being defiled, these men stayed outside the house where they had taken Jesus for trial—it*

Pilate:
The Roman governor Pilate oversaw Judea (the region where Jerusalem was located) A.D. 26–36. Pilate was unpopular with the Jews because he had taken money from the temple treasuries to build an aqueduct. Pilate resided in Caesarea, but he came to Jerusalem during the major feasts to handle any riots or insurrections that might take place.[†]

---

† Barton, B. B. (1993). *John* (pp. 363–364). Wheaton, IL: Tyndale House.

was not against the law to be in the courtyard or on a porch. They kept the ceremonial requirements of their religion while harboring murder and treachery in their hearts.[48]

The irony is rich, indeed. The religious leaders don't want to break their own ceremonial rules, but they are willing to kill Jesus. Keep in mind, nowhere in the Hebrew scriptures does it say that entering a Gentile home would defile a Jew; this is a man-made rule. John includes this nugget of information so that we can see the hypocrisy of religion—these men are willing to murder an innocent man but won't cross a threshold in order to keep their images intact.

What question does Pilate ask when he goes outside to meet the Jewish leaders (verse 29)?

Jesus' accusers are in a pickle. They have no charge that would stand up in a Roman court of law, and they know it. So, they do not answer Pilate's question directly; instead they give an allegation about Jesus' character.

What does Pilate tell them to do with Jesus (verse 31)?

It seems Pilate's number one motive is merely to keep the peace and prevent riots, which is why he agrees to have Jesus arrested. One scholar said that he was not interested in the "constant squabbling among the Jews, [and] was satisfied that this potential troublemaker was in custody."

What problem do the leaders confess to Pilate (verse 31)?

According to verse 32, why is it necessary that Jesus die by Roman execution?

Jesus predicted that He would die on a cross. Capital punishment for the Jews was by stoning and for the Romans by crucifixion. So because the Jews insist that Jesus be put to death, Pilate enters his headquarters again to interrogate Jesus one more time.

What important question does Pilate ask Jesus (verse 33)?

What does Jesus want to know in response (verse 34)?

Jesus wants to determine the real nature of Pilate's question. If it is a political question, then the answer is no. Jesus is not a political ruler, but yes, He is a King. One commentary makes this important distinction.

> *If Pilate was asking this question in his role as the Roman governor, he would have been inquiring whether Jesus was setting up a rebel government. But the Jews were using the word king to mean their religious ruler, the Messiah. Israel was a captive nation, under the authority of the Roman Empire. A rival king might have threatened Rome; a Messiah could have been a purely religious leader.*[49]

The Romans would zealously squash anyone attempting to overthrow their rule. What Pilate doesn't understand is that Jesus is indeed a king—the long-anticipated Messiah, who rules over the Kingdom of God. It is this kingdom that Jesus refers to, and He holds far more power and authority than Pilate can even begin to imagine.

> *The Lord has established his throne in the heavens, and his kingdom rules over all.*
>
> PSALM 103:19

How does Jesus describe His Kingdom (verse 36)?

When Jesus says, "my Kingdom is not of this world," He is referring to the Kingdom of God, which is the primary subject of all His teachings. He came to earth to usher in the reign of God in human hearts by rescuing captives from the domain (or kingdom) of darkness.

Satisfied with Jesus' answer, Pilate declares, "I find no guilt in him." This should have ended the matter. But even here, we see the sovereignty of God who works all things for our good and His glory. That includes Pilate's cowardice. Although Pilate knows Jesus is innocent, he lacks the courage to stand by his conviction in the face of opposition. He fears a riot that would threaten his position as governor. But again, we see the hand of God in the glove of history revealed in these events.

Jesus' sacrificial death is God's eternal plan to redeem us. I love how Peter, someone familiar with failure, explains Jesus' role as the perfect lamb of God:

> *You were not redeemed with perishable things like silver or gold from your futile way of life inherited from your forefathers, but with precious blood, as of a lamb unblemished and spotless, the blood of Christ. For He was foreknown before the foundation of the world but has appeared in these last times for thesake of you who through Him are believers in God, who raised Him from the dead and gave Him glory, so that your faith and hope are in God.*
> — 1 Peter 1:18–21

> *God made him who had no sin to be sin for us, so that in him we might become the righteousness of God.*
>
> 2 CORINTHIANS 5:21

Finally, read 2 Corinthians 5:21 (in the margin). Why does it matter that Jesus was sinless?

Adam and Eve's rebellion in the Garden of Eden brought sin into this world (Genesis 3:6). With it came death, just as God had warned them (Genesis 2:17), and as a result, all humanity is now born with a sinful nature (Romans 5:12–19).

In addition to putting a barrier between us and God, our sinful nature subjected us to both physical and spiritual death because "the wages of sin is death" (Romans 6:23). Now, in order for humans to be reconciled with God there must be forgiveness of sin, and "without the shedding of blood, there is no forgiveness" (Hebrews 9:22).

From the very beginning, God illustrated what must happen to cover our sin. When Adam and Eve sinned in the Garden, God clothed them with "garments of skin" (Genesis 3:21) by shedding the blood of an animal. This animal's death instead of Adam's was the first sacrifice. Although perfectly illustrating that sin requires death, the countless animal sacrifices provided only a temporary covering, as they had to be made again and again, and the blood of those animals could never completely take away sin (Hebrews 10:4, 11).

Then Jesus, the perfect Lamb of God, entered the human story. All the Old Testament sacrifices pointed forward to the "once for all" sacrifice of Jesus Christ (Hebrews 7:27; 10:10). The only way we are reconciled to a holy God is through a perfect offering, which we would not have had if Jesus Christ was not without sin.[50]

Therefore, we rejoice when we hear Pilate say, "I find no guilt in Him!"

Take a few minutes as you conclude your time in the Word to worship Jesus, the spotless Lamb.

Day 3: John 19:1-16

Crucifixion: *Prophecies foretold that the Messiah would die by crucifixion. Keep in mind that these were recorded over 700 years prior to the invention of crucifixion. Stoning was the penalty the Old Testament law prescribed for blasphemy, but Jesus had repeatedly indicated that He would die by being "lifted up" (John 3:14; 8:28; 12:32).*

A few years ago, I helped a friend move from San Antonio to Nashville. Along the 13-hour road-trip, she introduced me to a true-crime podcast, an investigation of an unsolved mystery. We got so hooked on the show that we didn't want to stop for any reason. However, we did take a break for a Dairy Queen Blizzard; after all, what road trip is complete without one?

If the scene we read today in John's Gospel were in a television drama or a true-crime podcast, we would be arriving at the most intense moment in the series. But friends, this isn't fiction. Instead, the details we read today are 100% historically accurate and the culmination of hundreds of years of prophecy.

Today we come to the moment, mere hours before Christ's death, when Jesus stands before a crowd in Jerusalem that decides His fate. They are faced with this question: What should they do with this man who claims to be God?

As we will see, the crowd chants one blood-curdling cry, "Crucify Him!" How ironic that just days before, a group welcomed Him into Jerusalem shouting, "Hosanna"—God save us!

These cries twisted together to form a crown of thorns. The plea, "God save us," and the mob's "crucify Him" come together in God's sovereign plan of redemption as Jesus takes center stage as the Savior of the World.

To recap where we are in this unfolding drama, Jesus was arrested in the Garden of Gethsemane and escorted to the home of the High Priest, where He stood trial. All four Gospels record elements of this Jewish religious trial: false witnesses, a barrage of questions, and finally, a death sentence.

One problem stood in their way—the Jewish leaders didn't have the authority to kill anyone. So, at the crack of dawn, Jesus was marched to the home of Pontius Pilate, the Roman governor, who declared that Jesus was innocent.

Pilate attempted several times to release Jesus. He remembered a tradition where the Romans allowed the Jews to release one prisoner during the Passover Feast as a symbol of their own release from slavery in Egypt. Pilate offered Barabbas, who was a robber, murderer, and rebel. Surely, Pilate assumed, the crowd will want to release Jesus, an innocent rabbi, instead of this convicted felon. But, given a choice, the crowd chose Barabbas!

All of this led to Christ's suffering. The horrifying way our Lord died is beyond comprehension. The Romans were brutal, and they specialized in capital punishment. Over our next two days of study, we will behold the anguish Jesus faced. As we read the text, I pray that we come to love Jesus more as we see the height and depth of His love poured out for us.

Read John 19:1–16.

According to verse 1, what punishment does Jesus endure? (See Word Study "Flogged" in margin)

Flogged:
A Roman flogging was a frightful punishment. The whip was braided from leather thongs and interlaced with lead balls and metal and bone spikes. The prisoner was usually tied to a column or stake. The severity was such that prisoners usually fainted and sometimes died under it. The whipping was applied to the back and chest. Each stroke cut into the quivering flesh until the veins and sometimes the entrails were laid bare.[†]

It's hard to comprehend an innocent man being beaten to the point of death. But this was "justice" in the Roman world. The accused was punished before innocence or guilt was determined. Although Pilate knew Jesus was innocent, he thought the flogging would appease the Jews.[51]

What happens to Jesus after He is flogged (verses 2–3)?

The One who breathed out the stars is now struck by the hands of ruthless men. Jesus humbly endures not only the physical pain but also the humiliation. The irony can't be missed here—the true King of Glory now wears a crown of thorns.

[†] Mills, M. S. (1999). The Life of Christ: A Study Guide to the Gospel Record (Mt 27:27–Jn 19:3). Dallas, TX: 3E Ministries.

Thorns are the perfect symbol of why He is suffering, as Warren Wiersbe explains:

> Sin had brought thorns and thistles into the world (Gen. 3:17–19), so it was only fitting that the Creator wear a crown of thorns as He bore the sins of the world on the cross. The very metal He had created and placed in the ground was used to make nails to pound through His hands and feet.[52]

In addition to the crown of thorns, the soldiers place a cloak on Jesus' body, which was worn by Roman generals. John makes a special note that this robe is purple, the color of royalty. Ruthlessly, the Roman soldiers mock Jesus and His claim to kingship.

Besides the robe and crown of thorns, what else do the soldiers do to Jesus (verse 3)?

When Pilate presents the beaten Christ to the crowds, what does he say about Jesus (verse 4)?

The Romans believed a criminal would confess to a crime just to end his suffering. So, after Jesus endures the flogging without any confession, Pilate presents the mangled Jesus to validate the severity of the examination.

What do the chief priests and others cry out when they see Jesus (verse 6)?

What does Pilate say to their demand (verse 6)?

What reason do the Jews give for demanding Jesus' death (verse 7)?

The Jews are so blinded by fear of losing their power that they can't see Jesus for who He is. Even though they know He performed countless miracles to validate His claim, they refuse to believe. Unbelief is a matter of the heart, not the intellect. Before we pass judgment, we must realize that the same hardening can happen to us. We too can become blinded to the majesty of Jesus. We can become so tempted to live for our own glory that we fail to recognize that life is not about us—it's about Him!

The religious leaders believed they had Biblical grounds to kill Jesus. According to Leviticus 24:16: "Anyone who blasphemes the name of the Lord must be put to death." Therefore, if anyone claimed equality with God, as Jesus did, it would certainly be blasphemy. Except in this case, there was one problem—Jesus was and is God. It wasn't blasphemous because it was true! They missed it!

How does Pilate react when he learns that Jesus claimed to be God?

Followers of Roman mythology believed in a multitude of gods. Therefore, when the Jews tell Pilate that Jesus claimed to be a god, he becomes fearful. And now he wants to determine: Who is this man?

What does Jesus do in the face of this new inquiry? (Verse 9)

Imagine the beaten and disfigured Christ, the Lamb of God, standing silent before this Roman governor. From the world's point of view, Pilate seems in command. Yet, from heaven's point of view,

> **Friend of Caesar:** This title was the highest honor Caesar conferred on someone. Rome's political landscape was cutthroat. Pilate could be dismissed on a whim, so he won't do anything to jeopardize his position. Pilate must choose between Jesus and his career. He chooses his career over Christ.

the One who holds "all things together" is in full control of His destiny. Pilate only has breath in his lungs because Jesus wills it!

What is Jesus' response to Pilate in verse 11?

What accusation do the Jewish leaders use to stop Pilate from releasing Jesus (verse 12)?

What is Pilate's next move (verse 13–14)?

What do the chief priests say in response to Jesus' being proclaimed King (verse 15)?

Write verse 16.

Jesus is the King of Glory who stood in our place—the innocent for the guilty. The events of Jesus' arrest, trial, and sentencing occur in rapid succession. One Bible scholar notes, "From the human standpoint, the trial of Jesus was the greatest crime and tragedy in history. From the divine viewpoint, it was the fulfillment of prophecy and the accomplishment of the will of God." [53]

I close today with the lyrics of one of my favorite worship songs, "Man of Sorrows" by Hillsong. As I've soaked in this scene of Jesus' suffering and humiliation, this song fills my heart and I pray it blesses yours.

*Man of sorrows, Lamb of God
By His own betrayed
The sin of man and wrath of God
Has been on Jesus laid*

*Silent as He stood accused
Beaten, mocked, and scorned
Bowing to the Father's will
He took a crown of thorns*

*Oh, that rugged cross, my salvation
Where Your love poured out over me
Now my soul cries out, "Hallelujah"
"Praise and honour unto Thee"
— "Man of Sorrows", Hillsong Worship*

Conclude your time in the Word by listening to "Man of Sorrows" on YouTube and praising Jesus, who wore the crown of thorns for you.

Day 4: John 19:19-30

I've traveled to Israel many times. Each trip to the Holy Land left a deep impression upon me. The Bible comes to life as you walk where Jesus walked. A few years ago, I led a group of women to Israel on a Bible study tour. Entering Jerusalem is always an emotional experience. Not only has it been the subject of thousands of years of political turmoil, but this is the place—the very soil—upon which Jesus walked, and the place where He gave His life for us.

We walked the Via Dolorosa, a narrow, stone path believed to be the route Jesus took to His crucifixion nearly 2000 years ago. It is also known as "The Way of the Cross" or "The Way of Sorrow" and is one of Christendom's most sacred sites. We walked from the stone pavement, where Jesus was sentenced to death, all the way to Golgotha, where Jesus hung on the cross.

Walking this sacred path in silence, I was struck by the vendors pressing in from every side, the noisy hustle and bustle of the city, and the narrow alleyways. This is a steep climb from the city up to the hill we call Calvary. I imagined the agony Jesus must have felt as He traversed those streets. Even as a somewhat fit woman, I found the journey challenging, without having the additional burden of carrying a heavy wooden beam or having been whipped to the point of death.

As I walked the Via Dolorosa, I imagined the people who witnessed Jesus carrying His cross. What if Barabbas was among the crowds? Remember, he was the man who was supposed to be dying that day, but the mob released him and sentenced Jesus instead. I just wonder if he witnessed Jesus' walk towards Golgotha and thought, "That should have been me!"

I also thought about the lame man whom Jesus healed at the Pool of Bethesda. The location of his miraculous healing was only minutes away from where Jesus carried His cross. I wonder if this man watched the One who gave him a new lease on life face His own death? I also thought about Mary, Jesus' mother. Did she follow along and watch her son suffer? Did she weep over the injustice and cry out to God to end His torture?

The man who carried His cross to Calvary died in the place of Barabbas. Friend, you and I are Barabbas. Our sin deserves condemnation, but because of Jesus, we are declared "not guilty." So, as we read the account of Christ's death, let's do so from the vantage point of those who have been set free because Jesus was crucified in our place.

Read John 19:17–30 and imagine you are an eyewitness to this moment.

What are your first impressions? What stands out to you?

Who are mentioned as eyewitnesses of this event?

We know much of the detail about that fateful day because of John, the beloved disciple who penned this Gospel. Of the four Gospel writers, John was the only eyewitness to the crucifixion. Therefore, his account contains details that are missing from the others.

John alone shares how Jesus lovingly entrusted Mary, His mother, to his care. He alone tells of two of Jesus' final sayings from the cross: "I thirst" and "It is finished." This Gospel alone tells us that Christ's side was pierced by a soldier's spear and that there came forth blood and water. Without the record we read today, so many pieces of Good Friday would be missing: pieces of information that are vital to our understanding of what Christ accomplished for us and how He fulfilled His mission as the Lamb of God.

All the details John shares are important, but let's take a closer look at a few of them.

What is the name of the place where Jesus is crucified (verse 17)?

What does John say in verse 18 to indicate how Jesus is killed?

Crucifixion is detailed in the New Testament and in other ancient documents. After the sentencing, the victim was first subjected to flogging, a punishment so severe that some died under it. In Jesus' case, the flogging occurred before the final sentencing, to evoke pity from the mob. As we learned, the crowd wanted blood.

Golgotha:
This means "Place of the Skull. This hill may have been called this because of its stony top or because it was shaped like a skull. "Golgotha" is the Hebrew word for "skull." The familiar name Calvary is derived from the Latin calvaria *(also meaning "skull").*†

---

† Barton, B. B. (1993). *John* (p. 375). Wheaton, IL: Tyndale House.

Soldiers Divided His Garments: *The Roman soldiers who performed the crucifixion divided the victim's clothes among themselves. Clothing was not a cheap commodity in those days as it is today. Thus, this was part of the "pay" the executioners received for performing their gruesome duties.*

Next, the horizontal bar of the cross was bound to the condemned man's back. He was then led through the city to crucifixion, accompanied by a centurion and four soldiers who made up the execution party. Finally, a sign describing the crime for which he was sentenced was carried before him.

What is written on the sign that hangs on Jesus' cross, indicating the crime He is being punished for (verse 19)?

According to historians, after arriving at the place of crucifixion, the victim was stripped of his clothes, which became the soldiers' property. The crossbar was then hoisted upward to rest upon the upright bar which had already been prepared to receive it. Next, the victim's hands were nailed in place. In most cases, the feet were also nailed to the cross. As a result, the victim could raise himself up from time to time, thereby alleviating the strain upon his arms and diaphragm. After hours or even days of such torture, the victim would die of shock, exposure, loss of blood, or suffocation.

What occurs after Jesus is crucified (verses 23–24)?

Roman soldiers were a brutal bunch, their character shaped by a culture of brutality. These men were jaded by years of war, bloodshed, and a civilization where torture was entertainment. One can only imagine how they enjoyed inflicting blows upon Jesus and delighted in His suffering. Not only did they rejoice in the death of an innocent, but they also played a game to determine the winner of His garment.

Which part of His clothing is not divided (verse 23)?

John makes special note to highlight the tunic, because this detail is a fulfillment of prophecy. Why are the Bible prophecies of Jesus Christ's death so important? Because they are powerful evidence that the Bible is the Word of God, and man could not have created this story. As we study Jesus' death, let's look at a few more of the prophecies that are fulfilled.

First, I will give the Old Testament prophecy that foretells the Messiah's death and then you record how it was fulfilled.

PROPHECY:
"Even my close friend, whom I trusted, he who shared my bread, has lifted up his heel against me." Psalm 41:9

Fulfillment: Mark 14:10; Matthew 26:14–16

PROPHECY
"He was despised and rejected by men, a man of sorrows, and familiar with suffering. Like one from whom men hide their faces, he was despised, and we esteemed him not." Isaiah 53:3

Fulfillment: Mark 14:65, Matthew 27:28–30

PROPHECY:
"He was oppressed and afflicted, yet he did not open his mouth; he was led like a lamb to the slaughter, and as a sheep before her shearers is silent, so he did not open his mouth." Isaiah 53:7

Fulfillment: Mark 15:5; John 19:9

PROPHECY:
"My God, my God, why have you forsaken me? Why are you so far from saving me, so far from the words of my groaning? O my God, I cry out by day, but you do not answer, by night, and am not silent." Psalm 22:1–2

Fulfillment: Matthew 27:46

PROPHECY:
"All who see me mock me; they hurl insults, shaking their heads: 'He trusts in the LORD; let the LORD rescue him. Let him deliver him, since he delights in him.'" Psalm 22:7–8

Fulfillment: Matthew 27:40, 44; Mark 15:32

PROPHECY:
"My strength is dried up like a potsherd, and my tongue sticks to the roof of my mouth; you lay me in the dust of death." Psalm 22:15

Fulfillment: Matthew 27:48

Now, in light of all these prophecies, read John 19:28–30. What words are the last spoken by Jesus on the cross (verse 30)?

This phrase in the original language is one word, *tetelestai*, which meant "it is accomplished," or "paid in full." This was an accounting term found on ancient documents, written over debts indicating that full payment was made. If you have a mortgage, you can imagine the relief of seeing the words "paid in full" written across that bill. This is what Jesus did for our debt of sin.

Read Romans 8:1–2 in the margin.

What is true of those who put faith in Christ?

> *There is therefore now no condemnation for those who are in Christ Jesus. For the law of the Spirit of life has set you free in Christ Jesus from the law of sin and death.*
> ROMANS 8:1–2

It is finished! Jesus' death accomplished our redemption. With Christ, the sacrificial system ended because Jesus took all sin upon himself. Now we are forgiven and can freely approach God because of what Jesus did for us.

Close your time in God's Word by expressing praise to Jesus who accomplished your redemption and frees us from condemnation!

Video Teaching Notes

Video teachings available for free at www.beholdandbelieve.com.

WEEK 8: BEHOLD, THE RESURRECTED KING

Jesus said to her, "I am the resurrection and the life. The one who believes in me will live, even though they die." — John 11:25

I. The Grand Narrative of the Bible; Genesis 2:7, Romans 5:12

It was in a garden, ages ago that paradise was lost, and it is in a garden now that it would be regained. — Ken Girl

II. Jesus and the Feasts of the Lord

Feast of Passover
Date: 14th day of Nisan

Commemorated:

Key Symbols:

Christ Fulfilled; Mark 14:12–26, John 19:18–37

Feast of Unleavened Bread; Exodus 12:15–20, Leviticus 23:5–8
Date: 15th day of Nisan

Commemorated:

Key Symbols:

Christ Fulfilled; Matthew 26:26, John 19:28–42

Jesus, the unleavened bread of God form Heaven, took on all our "leaven" of sin and was buried the exact same day the Jews had been celebrating this feast for centuries. While the Jewish people were removing the physical leaven from their homes, Jesus removed the spiritual leaven of sin from our house—that is, our life. — Dr. Richard Booker

Feast of First Fruits
Date: 17th day of Nisan (3 days after Passover)

Commemorated:

Key Biblical Events that occurred on this date:

Christ Fulfilled; John 20:20–21, Romans 8:11, 2 Corinthians 5:17

SMALL GROUP QUESTIONS

1. What did you behold about Jesus in your homework this week? What did this lead you to believe?
2. In today's teaching, Marian shared the Grand Narrative of the Bible. How does this view of Scripture enrich your faith?
3. Read the prophecy found in Isaiah 53. These words were penned hundreds of years before Christ was born and before crucifixion was even invented. Considering what you've learned about the Feasts of the Lord. What specifics did Isaiah prophesy that were fulfilled by Jesus' suffering, death, and resurrection?
4. Jesus rose from the grave on the Feast of First Fruits. According to John 11:25–26; 1 Thessalonians 4:13–18; and Romans 6:5–6, what does Jesus' resurrection promise to those who trust in Him?
5. We see in John 20:20–21 that Jesus breathed on the disciples the Holy Spirit. How does this event fulfill the His great mission to redeem what was lost in the Garden of Eden?
6. Read 2 Corinthians 5:17. What does this verse mean in light of all we've studied today?

WEEK 8

Day 1

Have you ever questioned, "How did we get here?" Perhaps you were in an argument and wondered what started the disagreement in the first place? Or perhaps you are a parent, and your child detoured down a path you didn't see coming. There are moments in life that cause us to pause and ask, "How did we get here?"

As we look at the broken body of Jesus we can't help but consider what led to this dark day. We could go back three years to when Jesus first entered public ministry at His baptism. We could then proceed to view His miracles, teachings, and proclamations of the Kingdom of God. After all, these glimpses of glory are what evoked the jealousy of the Jewish leaders and prompted their plot to kill Jesus.

But to start with Jesus' ministry would be an inaccurate understanding of His horrific death. For Scripture tells us that God ordained "before the foundation of the world" that His Son would come as the Perfect Lamb to take our place and provide forgiveness of sin (1 Peter 1:20). Therefore, to answer the question, "How did we get here?" we must go all the way back to the ancient battle that has raged since the dawn of time for the souls of man.

To grasp how we arrived at the death of Jesus, we must begin at the Garden of Eden. For it was there that God the Father made a promise to the serpent.

> So the Lord God said to the serpent:
> "Because you have done this,
> You are cursed more than all cattle,
> And more than every beast of the field;
> On your belly you shall go,
> And you shall eat dust

*All the days of your life.
And I will put enmity
Between you and the woman,
And between your seed and her Seed;
He shall bruise your head,
And you shall bruise His heel."
— Genesis 3:14–15 NKJV*

This is the first time God promised redemption. His promise centered on a "seed." How appropriate for a garden, right? But this seed was not of a plant, but "the Seed of a woman," meaning the offspring of a human being.

God promised that One would come from the lineage of Adam and Eve who would reverse the curse of sin by defeating the serpent. Sure, the serpent would wound Him (the Seed) on the heel, but He (the Seed) would crush the serpent's head!

Thus, we see that this Garden promise was fulfilled on the cross.

On that fateful Friday, as the sky turned black over Jerusalem, hell rejoiced because Satan thought he'd won. Satan worked through Judas' betrayal, the High Priests' jealousy, Pilate's fear, and through bloodthirsty soldiers to kill Jesus. And as Jesus said, "It is finished," the serpent wrongly believed he had rid the world of the Son of God.

Spoiler alert! Satan didn't win.

I am getting ahead of myself. The ultimate victory is still two days away. In today's passage, Jesus surrenders His spirit to death and His lifeless body is placed in a tomb. There are skeptics who argue that Jesus did not die on the cross. The text we read today gives ample historical evidence that the doubters are wrong. It's imperative to our faith that we know that Jesus did not faint, He did not enter into a coma, nor did He pretend to die. Jesus fully experienced death. As hard as the details are to digest, we need to face these facts so we can be fully confident that our Savior conquered the grave.

Read John 19:30–37.

What does Jesus do after saying "it is finished" (verse 30)?

Why do the Jews ask for the bodies to be removed from the cross (verse 31)?

Normally, the Romans left crucified bodies on the cross as a warning to others. But in this case, the Jews do not want the bodies hanging on the following Sabbath day, so they ask for Jesus' death to be quickened. They want His legs broken, a practice often done during crucifixion to make breathing difficult and cause death to come quickly.

What do the soldiers discover when they go to break Jesus' legs (verses 32–33)?

To confirm Jesus' death, what does the Roman soldier do (verse 34)?

John wants us to know that His testimony concerning Jesus' physical death is true. Why does John want us to know this (verse 35)?

Write verse 36.

These actions by the Roman soldiers fulfill specific Scripture about the Messiah's death. What two specific things does John note? (Verses 36–37)

WEEK 8

Read the following Old Testament Scriptures and note what is specifically fulfilled when Jesus dies.

Exodus 12:46 (This passage refers to the Passover Lamb.)

Zechariah 12:10 (This passage refers to the Messiah.)

I'll be Captain Obvious for a minute—we must remember that Jesus could not have orchestrated what happened to Him during death. He certainly couldn't control how He was buried. This is important to note because it increases our faith in the Word of God. John is adamant that we recognize this because our belief in Jesus is built upon this divine revelation. Fulfilled prophecy is proof that Jesus is who He claimed to be.

Now we come to a point in the story where we see two more significant prophecies fulfilled: Jesus' physical state at death, and where and how He is buried.

Read Isaiah 53:4–11.

How is Jesus' death depicted in this passage (verses 4–5)?

What other similarities to Jesus' death do you see in this prophecy?

The prophet Isaiah saw the Messiah "so disfigured beyond that of any man." Death by crucifixion was extreme torture, which left the victim completely unrecognizable.

Ken Gire describes how Jesus must have looked after His sufferings:

> *The body lies there, pathetically, in a twisted pose. His head is punctured from Jerusalem thorns. His face, swollen and discolored from Roman fists. His shoulders, pulled out of socket from the pendulous weight of the last six hours. His hands and feet—bored and rasped by seven-inch spikes—expose ragged muscles and white bone. His back and rib cage, clawed from a savage cat-o-nine tails.*[54]

I know this description is difficult to read, but I believe it's important to remember that the cost to redeem us was not cheap.

How does learning the details of Jesus' death help you appreciate His love for you more?

Before we leave Isaiah's prophecy, note how he described the Messiah's burial (verse 9).

Jesus' manner of death and His burial give vivid evidence to both the sovereignty of God and the truthfulness of Scripture. Hundreds of years before Jesus walked the earth, Isaiah also predicted that the Messiah would be buried in a rich man's tomb.

Read John 19:38–42.

Who are the two men who bury Jesus? Do you think they would be considered credible witnesses?

What specific care do they give to Christ's body?

Where is the tomb located (verse 41)?

Friends, we come again to a garden, an ironic place for a tomb unless God Himself is the author of this story. In a garden, seeds are planted into the earth. Likewise, Jesus' body is taken from the cross and placed inside a tomb. When a seed goes into the ground, it dies. And from that death comes the life of the plant. Thus, the mystery of Christ's death and resurrection is literally woven into the very fabric of nature. God has been illustrating the Gospel since the beginning of time. All creation bears witness to redemption!

Jesus is the Seed of the woman, the promised Redeemer in the Garden of Eden (Genesis 3:15). And He prophesied this reality about His own death:

> *I tell you the truth, unless a kernel of wheat is planted in the soil and dies, it remains alone. But its death will produce many new kernels—a plentiful harvest of new lives.*
> *— John 12:24 NLT*

A seed must die for the harvest to come.

The promise made to the serpent in the Garden of Eden was fulfilled by Christ's death on the cross. When Jesus' lifeless body was placed in a cold, dark grave, it seemed like Satan won, for the serpent had struck His heel.

Friend, what Satan intended for evil, our God used for good! Jesus' death paid the penalty for sin—past, present, and future. Everyone who places their faith in Jesus as their substitute is forgiven and free. On that cross, Jesus took on our debt and brought about the redemption of the world.

We leave today facing the darkness of death. But friends, Sunday is a comin'! And oh, what a glorious day it will be as we see King Jesus crush the serpent's head!

Take a few minutes to praise God for His perfect plan of redemption that unfolded from Garden to Garden.

Day 2: John 20:1-18

> "Grace is the only force in the universe powerful enough to break the chains that enslave generations."
>
> PHILIP YANCEY, WHAT'S SO AMAZING ABOUT GRACE?

It is dawn on Sunday when Mary Magdalene slips into the cold Jerusalem morning. Her destination is the garden tomb, where they had buried Jesus. Mary is a follower of Christ and part of the group that traveled with Him as He ministered. She was with His mother and the Apostle John standing near the cross as they watched Him die. And now, three days later, she would be the first to the tomb. The other disciples are too afraid to surface from hiding, but not Mary. She doesn't care; she has one thing on her mind—Jesus.

The Romans and the Jewish leaders have already taken away the one thing that mattered to her in the world—her Lord. As she runs towards the tomb—oh, just saying the word "tomb" causes her stomach to lurch—she remembers the first day she saw Him.

Jesus entered her village and her world turned upside down. Everyone had heard of Him, but now she would see the One whom many believed was the Messiah. As a little girl she'd been raised to believe that God would send a Deliverer. She'd always heard that the Messiah would make all things new. Every little Jewish boy and girl knew these words that were prophesied about their Messiah and waited in expectation for the One who would proclaim freedom for the captives!

When Jesus announced that He was the Messiah in his hometown of Nazareth, He read these words form the prophet Isaiah:

*The Spirit of the Sovereign Lord is on me,
because the Lord has anointed me
to proclaim good news to the poor.
He has sent me to bind up the brokenhearted,
to proclaim freedom for the captives
and release from darkness for the prisoners,
to proclaim the year of the Lord's favor
and the day of vengeance of our God,
to comfort all who mourn,
and provide for those who grieve in Zion—
to bestow on them a crown of beauty
instead of ashes,
the oil of joy
instead of mourning,
and a garment of praise
instead of a spirit of despair.
They will be called oaks of righteousness,
a planting of the Lord
for the display of his splendor.
— Isaiah 61:1–3*

Jesus said, "if the Son sets you free, you will be free indeed."
JOHN 8:36

Mary Magdalene had been a captive, possessed by seven demons (Luke 8:1). That was her claim to fame. Not one, not two, but seven demonic spirits tormented her. She was afflicted by an evil which left her hopeless for change. Her life was a walking billboard for Satan's schemes. Yet, within her was a kernel of faith that hoped for the Messiah who could release prisoners from darkness.

We aren't told how He healed her, we are just told that Mary encountered Jesus and was never the same again. From that moment on, she devoted her life to following Him. Words cannot express her adoration. Love born of gratitude.

- How can you not love the One who sets you free?
- How can you not love the One who healed your body, soul and spirit?
- How can you not love the One who extends acceptance when all you've known is rejection?

As she hurries towards the garden she sighs, likely thinking, "He cast seven demons out of me, yet didn't save His own life? I'm living proof that He had the power—why did He submit to such a death? It doesn't seem right."

Read John 20:1–9.

What does Mary discover at the garden tomb?

To whom does Mary run when she discovers the empty tomb?

Warren Wiersbe notes what happens next: "In her confusion and disappointment, Mary jumped to conclusions and thought someone had stolen Christ's body. She ran to tell Peter and John, who in turn visited the tomb."[55]

When the disciples race to the grave and look inside, what specific details do they see (verses 5–7)?

When John (the other disciple with Peter) looks inside the tomb and sees the evidence, what happens (verse 8)?

What happens to John in that empty tomb? Warren Wiersbe writes "John saw the burial wrappings lying in the shape of the body, but the body was gone! The graveclothes lay like an empty cocoon. The napkin (for the face) was carefully folded, lying by itself. It was not the scene of a grave robbery, for no robbers could have gotten the body out of the graveclothes without tearing the cloth and disarranging things. Jesus had returned to life in power and glory and had passed through the graveclothes and the tomb itself!" [56]

Although many will accuse them of fabricating this story about the resurrection, their testimonies show that, in fact, they are surprised that Jesus is not in the tomb. When John sees the graveclothes looking like an empty cocoon from which Jesus had emerged, it is then that he believes that Jesus had risen.[57]

What do Peter and John do after witnessing the empty tomb (verse 10)?

> "It was in a garden, ages ago that paradise was lost, and it is in a garden now that it would be regained."
>
> KEN GIRE

Although the men go home, Mary doesn't budge. She stands outside the tomb crying. The events of the past few days have caught up with her. She must have been in shock from watching the brutality of His death, but now with His body missing a flood of grief pours out. With hot tears streaming down her cheeks, Mary bends over to look in the tomb and sees two angels seated where Jesus' body had been. Friend, God writes the best stories! The woman once possessed by demons is now greeted by angels.

Read John 20:11–18.
What do the angels ask Mary (verse 13)?

As she leaves the angelic conversation, whom does she encounter?

What question does Jesus also ask her (verse 15)?

With whom does Mary first assume she's talking (verse 15)?

What strikes me about this scene is how both the angels and Jesus are perplexed as to why Mary is grieving. It's as if they can't even comprehend why she is crying, because they assumed Christ's resurrection was obvious. And it should have been expected! Jesus told the disciples time and time again what would occur.

According to Matthew 16:21 in the margin, what had Jesus predicted?

> *From that time Jesus began to show his disciples that he must go to Jerusalem and suffer many things from the elders and chief priests and scribes, and be killed, and on the third day be raised.*
>
> MATTHEW 16:21

Jesus has every right to play the "I told you so" card. His track record for keeping His promises is 100%. But Mary still hasn't clued into what is happening. Keep in mind, the last time she saw Jesus, His body was brutalized beyond recognition. Truly, it seems the last person she's anticipating in that garden is her Lord. Although Mary isn't expecting Him, something happens that would turn her mourning into dancing.

What does Jesus say to her in John 20:16?

What does Mary do immediately after hearing her name?

What do the following scriptures reveal about God calling His own by name? Isaiah 43:1, John 10:3–4

Why do you think this has such an impact on Mary?

WEEK 8

She knows that voice! This is Jesus! Although she watched Him die, He is now very much alive! Once that realization sinks in, she flings herself at Him! *The Bible Guide Commentary* explains,

> *When Mary realizes that this is Jesus, she exclaims, "Rabboni"—the Aramaic word for "greatest teacher," or "my teacher and God." She wants to hold fast to him, to prevent him ever going away again. He gently tells her that he is returning to his Father. Just as he laid down his life, he is now taking it up again.[58]*

Loosening her hold, Jesus commissions the woman who was once defeated by demons to be the first proclaimer of His victory.

What instruction does Jesus give Mary (verse 17)?

What does Mary proclaim to the disciples (verse 18)?

What does it tell you about Jesus that the first proclaimer of the resurrection is a formerly demon-possessed woman?

Jesus chooses an unlikely witness to be the first person to testify of His resurrection. But Mary's testimony would not be the last. Over the next forty days, 500 different people would be eyewitnesses of the Risen Christ.

How is your faith strengthened by the knowledge that the resurrection was witnessed by so many?

I don't think Jesus first appears to Mary because she is the best candidate. Instead, I believe Jesus appears to her because she, of all people, needs to know that darkness didn't win. Mary is overcome with grief partly because she had buried her hope. But on that first Easter day, her mourning turns to dancing because Jesus won!

Conclude your time in the Word by worshipping the Risen Christ. Take time to contemplate what His victory over sin and death truly means for your life.

Day 3: John 20:19-31

Yesterday we experienced the resurrection from Mary Magdalene's perspective. We felt her heartache and then her ecstatic joy at seeing Jesus alive. Today we consider how the other disciples must have felt. The last time we've seen most of them was in the Garden of Gethsemane, the night of Jesus' arrest. Since then, they've been hiding for fear of their own lives. So, it's easy to imagine that the news of the resurrection sent them on a roller-coaster of emotions too.

From Friday until Sunday morning, the only thing the disciples knew was that Jesus' body was in a tomb, and a massive stone blocked the entrance. When that stone sealed Jesus' grave, it effectively crushed their hopes and left them disillusioned. While it is easy for us, two thousand years later, to rejoice, we must consider the fact that the disciples didn't have our knowledge as they huddled in fear. They were in trauma and had to wrap their minds around all that was unfolding.

To illustrate how the disciples must have felt in the time lapse, Dr. James Boice offers this incredible story about the Battle of Waterloo, which occurred between England and France. At the end of the battle, England waited to learn if their leader, Wellington, had won or lost to Napoleon. For a while they believed the worst, but learning the truth changed everything!

> At the conclusion of the Battle of Waterloo, there were no telegrams or radio sets in those days, but everyone knew that a great battle was pending, and they were anxious to hear what would happen when Wellington, the British general, faced Napoleon. A signalman was placed on the top of Winchester Cathedral with instructions to keep his eye on the sea. When he received a message, he was to pass the message on to another man on a hill. That man was to pass it to another. And so it was to go until news of the battle was finally relayed to London and then across England.
>
> At length a ship was sighted through thick fog on the English Channel. The signalman on board sent the first word—"Wellington."
>
> The next word was "defeated."
> Then fog prevented the ship from being seen.
> "Wellington defeated!"
>
> The message was sent across England, and gloom descended over the countryside. After two or three hours the fog lifted, and the signal came again: "Wellington defeated the enemy!" Then England rejoiced.
>
> In the same way, Jesus' death plunged his friends into sadness. It was an apparent defeat. But on the third day he rose again in victory. When Jesus died men might have cried, "Christ is defeated, wrong has triumphed, sin has won." But after three days the fog lifted, and the full message came through to the world: "Jesus is risen; he has defeated the enemy."[59]

> "We have to put ourselves in the frame of mind of the disciples between the afternoon of Jesus' crucifixion and the morning of his resurrection, and that is not easy to do. Our experience of Easter is one of faith and joy. But in the days that elapsed between Christ's death and resurrection, those who were closest to him were filled with the deepest disillusionment and gloom." [†]
>
> JAMES BOICE

[†] Boice, J. M. (2005). *The Gospel of John: an expositional commentary* (pp. 1569–1570). Grand Rapids, MI: Baker Books.

Let's open the Gospel of John and behold the moment the "fog lifts" for the disciples and they absorb the truth of Jesus' victory over sin and death.

Read John 20:19–23.

Where are the disciples and what are they doing (verse 19)?

Why do you think Jesus repeatedly speaks "peace" over the disciples?

Raise your hand if you've ever been so afraid that you locked your doors and moved a piece of furniture in front of it. Guilty! This is exactly how I imagine this scene. The disciples have come together, bolted the door, and begin to compare notes, and Jesus suddenly appears among them. They are baffled, and some think they've seen a ghost.

Piecing together the different Gospel accounts of what occurs on this first Easter Sunday, we see that Jesus is quite busy. First, He appears to Mary Magdalene and sends her to tell the disciples of His resurrection. Then He appears to the other women and next, we learn from Luke's Gospel that He also appears to two disciples who are going to a village called Emmaus. Take a minute to read this account, which sheds light on the disciple's state after hearing of Jesus' resurrection.

Read Luke 24:13–36.

How do the two disciples describe "Jesus of Nazareth" (verse 19)?

WEEK 8

What is their hope (verse 21)?

What news do they report to this mysterious person (verses 22–24)?

What does Jesus teach these disciples as they walk along the road (verses 25–27)?

When do the disciples recognize that this is Jesus (verses 30–32)?

What physical act does Jesus do that proves He is not a ghost?

As you noted in your initial reading, Jesus speaks the word "peace" over His disciples multiple times. Obviously, they've had a whirlwind of emotions and now they are a bit shocked to see Him appear inside bolted doors. One scholar makes this observation:

> *The appearance of Jesus in the room excited both amazement and fear. The implication is clear that Jesus was not impeded by locked doors. The resurrection body has properties different from the body of flesh; yet it is not ethereal.*[60]

> And Jesus came and said to them, "All authority in heaven and on earth has been given to me. Go therefore and make disciples of all nations, baptizing them in the name of the Father and of the Son and of the Holy Spirit, teaching them to observe all that I have commanded you. And behold, I am with you always, to the end of the age."
>
> MATTHEW 28:18–20

What evidence does Jesus offer to prove His identity (John 20:20)?

How do the disciples feel (emotion) after seeing Christ's hands and feet?

How does this fulfill the promise Jesus made to them in John 16:20–22?

Looking again at our focal passage, write what Jesus said in John 20:21.

Just as Jesus came from Heaven to earth to offer salvation, so we are sent into the world with the Gospel. Review Matthew 28:18–20 in the margin and record what you learn about our mission.

To equip the disciples for this mission, what does Jesus do next? (John 20:22)

What similarities do you see between verse John 20:22 and Genesis 2:7?

Here we come full circle. Just as God breathed physical life into Adam, so Christ breathes spiritual life into the disciples. The Holy Spirit gives us resurrection life. Recall Jesus' words to Nicodemus. (See side bar.)

Read John 20:24–31.

What testimony do the disciples share with Thomas?

What does Thomas say he needs to believe in the resurrection (verse 25)?

When Jesus appears to the group again, what specific instructions does He give Thomas (verse 27)? What does this imply about Jesus?

What is Thomas' response to this evidence (verse 28)? What do you think Thomas means by this exclamation?

What does Jesus say about those who believe without seeing Him (verse 29)?

What does John explain in verses 30–31?

Jesus answered, "Truly, truly, I say to you, unless one is born of water and the Spirit he cannot enter into the kingdom of God. That which is born of the flesh is flesh, and that which is born of the Spirit is spirit. Do not be amazed that I said to you, 'You must be born again.' The wind blows where it wishes and you hear the sound of it, but do not know where it comes from and where it is going; so is everyone who is born of the Spirit."

JOHN 3:5–8

> Faith is "the substance of things hoped for, the evidence of things not seen."
> HEBREWS 11:1

Thomas moves from doubting to professing faith in a fraction of a second. Just one touch of Jesus' nail-scarred hands sealed the deal. But Jesus says that it is far better for those who exercise faith without sight. As Hebrews 11:6 says, "Without faith it is impossible to please him, for whoever would draw near to God must believe that he exists and that he rewards those who seek him."

Thomas's proclamation of faith serves as the climax of John's Gospel. All the miraculous signs, the "I Am" statements, the unfolding drama of Jesus' arrest, and His sacrificial death led to this one critical moment of decision. What will we do with Jesus Christ?

John confesses he has many more details which he could have shared, but his primary motive for writing is that we would believe in Jesus and experience eternal life.

Without the resurrection, our faith is empty. This leads me to share one of the greatest pieces of evidence we have for it. In his book, *The Case for Christ*, journalist Lee Strobel interviewed historian Dr. J.P. Moreland and asked him, "As a historian and a philosopher, can you share with me what are the greatest pieces of evidence for the resurrection?" Dr. Moreland responded:

> For since we believe that Jesus died and rose again, we also believe that God will bring with Jesus those who have fallen asleep in Him.
> 1 THESSALONIANS 4:14

First of all, you have to consider the transformation of the disciples. Think about this. By Good Friday, when Christ was crucified, almost all of Jesus' apostles had deserted him. They had scurried away like rats off a sinking ship. They did not want to be accused along with the Lord. They did not want to suffer His same fate, so they deserted Him. Yet three days later, these timid, cowardly disciples were transformed into courageous, bold defenders of the Christian faith. Most of them gave up their lives for the truth of Jesus Christ.

> *Nobody willingly dies for a lie that they know is a lie. Jesus' disciples were willing to die for the truth of the resurrection because they knew it was the truth. The reason they died for the Lord Jesus Christ is they had seen the risen Christ themselves. That's what transformed them. Therefore, the most significant proof for resurrection is the transformation of the disciples.*[61]

Friend, our faith is built on a solid foundation. We can have hope in this life and for eternity because He lives! This is not a fable, but a fact that men and women were willing to die for because the resurrection is true.

> *If you were to stand trial for your faith in Jesus, how would you answer the question: Why do you believe?*

The resurrection is a historical fact, and it was the moment that all of Heaven awaited. Hands down, my favorite worship song of all time is "King of Kings" by Hillsong. I truly embarrass myself, and others I might add, when we sing it in church. This one line gets me every time!

> *And the morning that You rose*
> *All of Heaven held its breath*
> *'Til that stone was moved for good*
> *For the Lamb had conquered death!*

Conclude your time of studying God's Word by worshipping the resurrected King Jesus. Listen to "King of Kings" by Hillsong and worship the One who conquered death!

Day 4: John 21

> *"The gospel is about living in the light of Jesus' resurrection power every day. It's about who we trust in every moment with our life and eternity."*
>
> LOUIE GIGLIO,
> THE COMEBACK

I worked at a summer camp back in my college years. Brutal, hot days were followed by prank-filled nights, culminating in memories that lasted a lifetime. At the end of each two-week session, parents arrived to pick up their kiddos. Then counselors, campers, and parents piled into the gym as we said goodbye with a closing ceremony. With sweaty arms wrapped around each other, we hugged tight and wiped our eyes as over the loudspeaker played, "Friends are Friends Forever." Swaying to this camp classic, we concluded our adventure with a few awards, some long goodbyes, and promises to see each other again next year.

Today feels like the closing ceremony for our study. I'm about to cry, just thinking about it. So, if you'll permit me a little bit of a sappy goodbye, I'd like to tell you how much I've enjoyed these days in God's Word with you. My prayer is that you've grown to love Jesus more as you've beheld His glory. I hope you walk away from Garden to Garden knowing that the Bible is one redemption story. It began with creation and will culminate with restoration when God makes all things new. At the center of it all stands the cross, where Jesus, the Lamb of God, laid down His life for you.

John concludes his Gospel with an epilogue that reminds us of three essential truths about Jesus—truths, I believe, he wants us to tuck away in our hearts and keep with us as we follow Christ in our daily lives.

Truth #1: Only Jesus Christ provides the abundant life.
Truth #2: Only Jesus Christ offers redeeming grace.
Truth #3: Only Jesus Christ is worthy of our very lives.

Our study today opens in a new setting. The disciples are no longer in Jerusalem, the scene of Christ's death and resurrection. Now they are back in Galilee, where Jesus said He would meet them. So, we find these followers of Christ back where it all started, fishing by the Sea of Galilee.

WEEK 8

There are seven men in a boat: Peter, Thomas, Nathanael, John (our author), his brother James, and two other unnamed disciples. Let's consider all they experienced over the past three years. First, they left everything to follow Jesus, and I do mean everything. For example, John left his father Zebedee's successful fishing business to be with Jesus, in addition to leaving friends, family, and his home. The others made their own significant sacrifices. And now, they return to the very place where they heard Jesus say, "Follow me."

Nothing prepared these men for all that they experienced. Sure, they witnessed miracles. But oh, so much more. They beheld Jesus. These disciples witnessed the "Word of God" manifested in flesh and blood. Yes, He was a man like them, but He was also the heaven-sent Son of God.

- They beheld the One who spoke creation into existence.
- They walked with the One who could walk on water.
- They ate their meals with the One who is the Bread of Life.
- They sat beside a fire with the One who appeared to Moses in the burning bush and said, "I AM!"
- They thought they were leaving their homes to follow a Rabbi, but what they discovered was the God of Glory!

Read John 21:1–8

What is the result of their night of fishing (verse 3)?

What question does Jesus ask them (verse 5)?

What does Jesus encourage them to do (verse 6)?

In verse 7, we see that John discerns that the man on the distant shore is Jesus. What does Peter do when he hears John's words?

Why do you think Peter is so eager to get to Jesus?

John shares this story to remind us of two things: first, the sheer emptiness of life apart from Christ; second, the lengths to which Jesus goes to show us grace.

Notice that these professional fishermen were out all night and have nothing to show for their efforts. Not one single fish! Their empty fishing net is symbolic of life apart from Christ.

When the stranger on the shore asks if they have any fish, the disciples have to answer sadly, "No." They have to admit they are failures. Friend, this is the place we all must come to in our lives—we must recognize our emptiness apart from Christ. We can try in our own strength, but at the end of the day, our nets are still empty without Him.

James Boice writes, "This is what Jesus asks us when we have been trying life on our own terms. 'Have you caught anything? Have you been successful? Are you satisfied?' He asks these questions so that we might recognize our hunger, need, and failure, and turn to Him."[62]

I was in a bar, holding an empty martini glass when the words of U2's song "I Still Haven't Found What I'm Looking For" pierced my heart. In that sliver of a second, I recognized my own emptiness and that I was desperately attempting to find life and love in all the wrong places. Sitting there in the darkness of a bar, surrounded by smoke and neon lights, I whispered a prayer, "God help me." And that one prayer changed everything. Friend, I've experienced life with Jesus and life without Him and I can tell you from first-hand experience—Jesus is better!

Throughout this Gospel, John has shown us miracle after miracle where Jesus provided abundantly. His miracles speak to His wonder-working power to fill the empty, heal the broken, and defeat the darkness. Start with the very first one, where Christ turned water into wine. Not only did Christ transform the water, but He provided enough wine for 10 weddings! Then we have the miraculous feeding of the 5,000, where Jesus took one boy's small lunch and multiplied it to feed thousands, with baskets of food left over.

The contrast of emptiness and abundance is John's primary point in this section. We can experience the abundant life with Jesus or an empty life without Him. John drives this point home by showing that the catch of fish that day is so large that seven men struggle to get it to shore.

> *Jesus said, "The thief comes only to steal and kill and destroy. I came that they may have life and have it abundantly."*
> JOHN 10:10

Read John 10:10 (in the margin). What does Jesus say He came to give us?

This story is more than just a spiritual reminder; it is flashback in time for one person in particular. What occurs in John 21 is an exact repeat of the miracle which happened three years prior when Jesus first called Peter to follow Him.

Read Luke 5:1–11.
What is similar about these two fishing events?

What does Jesus invite Peter to do after the miraculous catch of fish (verses 10–11)?

Returning to John 21, much has transpired since Peter left everything to follow Christ. The man who now jumps into the water carries tremendous shame. After all, Peter denied even knowing

Jesus. But when he sees Christ standing on the shore, Peter runs to Him. And guess what he finds? Grace. Peter experienced God's undeserved mercy.

Read John 21:9–19.

What does Jesus cook the disciples for breakfast?

What does this simple act tell you about God?

How do you think the disciples feel as Jesus fries them fish?

John specifically mentions the type of fire Jesus uses. What is it (verse 9)?

Please don't miss this! Back in John 18, when we studied Peter's denial, I asked you to note the type of fire that he sat beside. Yep, you guessed it, it was a "charcoal fire." Only twice in the Bible is that term used. Once, when Peter denied Jesus, and the other is here, when Jesus offers him grace.

I believe Jesus intentionally reenacts both scenes from Peter's life: first, Peter's calling with the miraculous catch of fish and then, his three-fold denial by the charcoal fire.

What questions does Jesus ask Peter after their breakfast (verse 15–17)?

How does Peter respond to these questions?

How does Jesus encourage Peter to prove or exhibit his love (verses 15–17)?

What two-word request does Jesus give Peter in verse 19? Where and when did Peter hear this before?

Because Jesus loves Peter, He offers him a chance to repent. Jesus' questions probe to the heart, causing His friend to reflect and grieve his past sin. True repentance is more than just being sorry we were busted; it is a recognition that our sin was against God and hurt our relationship. Therefore, for each denial, Peter is given an opportunity to profess His devotion. Jesus asks Peter three times, "Do you love me?" When Peter answers "yes," Jesus tells him to "feed His sheep."

It is one thing to say we love Jesus, but the real test requires doing it. Loving Christ is serving Him. Yes, Peter had repented, but here Jesus invites him to commit his life again to following Him. I believe Jesus asks these questions publicly, in front of the other disciples, so that they would know that Peter's past is in the past and that he is restored to leadership.

Peter leaves this conversation a transformed man, one who goes on to lead the early Church as a bold witness for Christ. Brokenness over sin produces the best leaders. God can truly use people once they recognize their utter dependence on Christ and when they can empathize with the weakness in others. So, Jesus cooks Peter breakfast to offer him the grace he desperately needs, to speak the truth that leads to repentance, and to remind him that he still has an important role to play in the Kingdom.

Read John 21:20–25.

Jesus warns Peter in verses 18–19 that he will eventually be arrested and killed because of his witness for Christ. What does Peter want to know after he's told this (verse 21)?

What command does Jesus give Peter again in response to his question (verse 22)?

What does John tell us in verse 25?

The hardest part of teaching the Bible is determining what content to leave out. Honestly, this Gospel is filled with so many revelations of Jesus that I'm frustrated by the limitations of time and paper. This is how John, the Beloved Disciple, must have felt. He shares this reality when he says in verse 25, "the world itself could not contain the books that would be written" about Jesus.

Truly, the world cannot contain the testimonies about Christ because the stories of transformed lives continue to grow daily. For the past two thousand years, as the Gospel has spread across the globe, men and women have come to know Jesus. And as they follow Him, their lives are touched by the One who turned water into wine, and they experience in their own hearts the miracle-working Messiah. These transformation stories could fill every library in the world!

Friend, your redemption story is part of this great library of faith! I pray you will tell the world about Jesus—His sacrificial death for sin and His resurrection life for victory. I pray your life showcases His glory as you follow Him, the Good Shepherd, wherever He leads.

Conclude your time in the Word by praising God for the things He's revealed to you about Himself in this study.

BEHOLD
AND
BELIEVE

Video Teaching Notes

Video teachings available for free at www.beholdandbelieve.com.

WEEK 9: BEHOLD, AND BELIEVE

For this is the will of My Father, that everyone who beholds the Son and believes in Him will have eternal life, and I Myself will raise him up on the last day. — John 6:40

I. BEHOLD

The next day he saw Jesus coming toward him, and said, "Behold, the Lamb of God, who takes away the sin of the world!" — John 1:29

So Jesus came out, wearing the crown of thorns and the purple robe. Pilate said to them, "Behold the man!" — John 19:5

Then the other disciple, who had reached the tomb first, also went in, and he saw and believed. — John 20:8

II. BELIEVE

That which was from the beginning, which we have heard, which we have seen with our eyes, which we looked upon and have touched with our hands, concerning the word of life— the life was made manifest, and we have seen it, and testify to it and proclaim to you the eternal life, which was with the Father and was made manifest to us— that which we have seen and heard we proclaim also to you, so that you too may have fellowship with us; and indeed our fellowship is with the Father and with his Son Jesus Christ. And we are writing these things so that our joy may be complete. — 1st John 1:1–4

These are written that you may believe that Jesus is the Messiah, the Son of God, and that by believing you may have life in his name. — John 20:30

Believe me that I am in the Father and the Father is in me, or else believe on account of the works themselves. "Truly, truly, I say to you, whoever believes in me will also do the works that I do; and greater works than these will he do, because I am going to the Father." — John 14:11–12

Then Jesus told him, "Because you have seen me, you have believed; blessed are those who have not seen and yet have believed." — John 20:29

SMALL GROUP QUESTIONS

1. What did you behold about Jesus in your homework this week? What did this lead you to believe?
2. How is "beholding" Jesus different than simply seeing or recognizing Him?
3. Read 1st John 1:1-4. Share a few things that John the Apostle witnessed as a disciple that transformed him for eternity.
4. What was John's clear objective in writing this Gospel? John 20:30.
5. Read John 6:40. What is the Father's desire? What does Jesus promise to do for those who believe?
6. How did God use this study of the Gospel of John in your life?

DEDICATION

Behold and Believe is lovingly dedicated to my beautiful friend, Becky Surber.

I consider our precious friendship a divine assignment and gift from the Lord. You are my Barnabas and I'm forever grateful. Thank you for all you've done to champion *Behold and Believe*. Without your vision, prayers, and persistence, this study of John's Gospel would not be in women's hands today. I am honored to serve Jesus, the Kingdom, and the women of Mission City Church alongside you.

ACKNOWLEDGEMENTS

To the women of **The Altar at Mission City Church: YOU DID THIS!** *Behold and Believe* was birthed out of our Tuesday mornings together. I'll never forget the day you surprised me with the check to publish this study so that we could put the Gospel of John into the hands of women across the globe. Your prayers, encouragement, and financial sacrifices made this publication possible. I'm forever grateful!

To my Pastors, Matt Surber and Don Long. It's an absolute honor to serve under your leadership at Mission City. Thank you for believing in this Bible study and empowering me to do what I love most—tell women about Jesus.

To my precious friend, Sarah Thompson. Thank you for reading and editing every single word of this study! Your feedback was so helpful and needed. You've been by my side with Chick-Fil-A sweet tea and grilled nuggets the entire publishing process. I love that our kids are growing up together, watching their mommas love and serve Jesus. I can't wait to read your book one day!

To the Board of Directors of *This Redeemed Life*. Your wisdom and prayers fuel me to do the work God has called me to do.

To the incomparable Whitney Gossett and the entire team at *Content Capital*. You guys are the best of the best, and you are stuck with me for life.

To my parents, Buddy and Susie Jordan. Your example of unshakeable faith and unwavering commitment to the Kingdom of God is the best thing you've given your children.

To Andrew, Brenden, and Sydney. I love you so much, and my prayer is that you never stop beholding the glory of God in the face of Christ. Jesus is better!

To Justin Ellis. I don't know where to begin to thank you and acknowledge the gift you are to the Kingdom of God. You are selfless, patient, wildly creative, and crazy detail-oriented. There is only one you on this planet, and I'm the incredibly blessed woman who gets to call you mine. Thank you for the countless (literally) hours you've set in front of a computer, making my words and teachings come to life in such a beautiful way. I don't deserve you, and that's a fact.

To my Jesus, the One and Only. You rescued my life from the pit, and I live to declare your praise!

ENDNOTES

1. Barton, B. B. (1993). *John* (pp. viii–ix). Wheaton, IL: Tyndale House.
2. Wiersbe, W. W. (1996). *The Bible exposition commentary* (Vol. 1, p. 284). Wheaton, IL: Victor Books.
3. Carpenter, E. E., & Comfort, P. W. (2000). In *Holman treasury of key Bible words: 200 Greek and 200 Hebrew words defined and explained* (p. 249). Nashville, TN: Broadman & Holman Publishers.
4. Boice, J. M. (2005). *The Gospel of John: an expositional commentary* (pp. 112–113). Grand Rapids, MI: Baker Books.
5. Boice, J. M. (2005). Ibid. (p. 151). Grand Rapids, MI: Baker Books.
6. Boice, J. M. (2005). Ibid. (pp. 165–166). Grand Rapids, MI: Baker Books.
7. Wiersbe, W. W. (1996). *The Bible exposition commentary* (Vol. 1, pp. 294–295). Wheaton, IL: Victor Books.
8. Keller, T. J. (2013). The Timothy Keller Sermon Archive. New York City: Redeemer Presbyterian Church.
9. Wiersbe, W. W. (1996). *The Bible exposition commentary* (Vol. 1, p. 296). Wheaton, IL: Victor Books.
10. White, J. E. (1998). John. In D. S. Dockery (Ed.), *Holman concise Bible commentary* (pp. 469–470). Nashville, TN: Broadman & Holman Publishers.
11. White, J. E. (1998). John. In D. S. Dockery (Ed.), Ibid. (p. 470). Nashville, TN: Broadman & Holman Publishers.
12. Boice, J. M. (2005). *The Gospel of John: an expositional commentary* (p. 272). Grand Rapids, MI: Baker Books.
13. Boice, J. M. (2005). Ibid. (p. 274). Grand Rapids, MI: Baker Books.
14. Barton, B. B. (1993). *John* (p. 96). Wheaton, IL: Tyndale House.
15. Wiersbe, W. W. (1992). *Wiersbe's expository outlines on the New Testament* (p. 223). Wheaton, IL: Victor Books.
16. Barton, B. B. (1993). *John* (pp. 102–103). Wheaton, IL: Tyndale House.
17. Carpenter, E. E., & Comfort, P. W. (2000). In *Holman treasury of key Bible words: 200 Greek and 200 Hebrew words defined and explained* (p. 157). Nashville, TN: Broadman & Holman Publishers.
18. Barry, J. D., Mangum, D., Brown, D. R., Heiser, M. S., Custis, M., Ritzema, E., ... Bomar, D. (2012, 2016). *Faithlife Study Bible* (Jn 5:1–18). Bellingham, WA: Lexham Press.
19. https://www.josh.org/jesus-liar-lunatic-lord/
20. Morris, L. (1995). *The Gospel according to John* (pp. 303–304). Grand Rapids, MI: Wm. B. Eerdmans Publishing Co.
21. Boice, J. M. (2005). *The Gospel of John: an expositional commentary* (p. 603). Grand Rapids, MI: Baker Books.
22. Barton, B. B. (1993). *John* (p. 173). Wheaton, IL: Tyndale House.
23. Boice, J. M. (2005). Ibid. (p. 626). Grand Rapids, MI: Baker Books.
24. Boice, J. M. (2005). Ibid. (p. 629). Grand Rapids, MI: Baker Books.
25. Barton, B. B. (1993). *John* (p. 179). Wheaton, IL: Tyndale House.
26. Osbeck, K. W. (1996). *Amazing grace: 366 inspiring hymn stories for daily devotions* (p. 170). Grand Rapids, MI: Kregel Publications.
27. Morris, L. (1995). *The Gospel according to John* (p. 440). Grand Rapids, MI: Wm. B. Eerdmans Publishing Co.
28. Wiersbe, W. W. (1992). *Wiersbe's expository outlines on the New Testament* (p. 237). Wheaton, IL: Victor Books.
29. Wiersbe, W. W. (1996). *The Bible exposition commentary* (Vol. 1, p. 332). Wheaton, IL: Victor Books.
30. Tenney, M. C. (1981). "John". In F. E. Gaebelein (Ed.), *The Expositor's Bible Commentary: John and Acts* (Vol. 9, p. 121). Grand Rapids, MI: Zondervan Publishing House.
31. Tenney, M. C. (1981). Ibid. (Vol. 9, p. 122). Grand Rapids, MI: Zondervan Publishing House.
32. Barton, B. B. (1993). *John* (p. 241). Wheaton, IL: Tyndale House.
33. Boice, J. M. (2005). *The Gospel of John: an expositional commentary* (pp. 916–917). Grand Rapids, MI: Baker Books.
34. Boice, J. M. (2005). Ibid. (p. 917). Grand Rapids, MI: Baker Books.
35. Boice, J. M. (2005). Ibid. (pp. 918–919). Grand Rapids, MI: Baker Books.
36. Wiersbe, W. W. (1996). *The Bible exposition commentary* (Vol. 1, p. 342). Wheaton, IL: Victor Books.
37. Tenney, M. C. (1981). "John". In F. E. Gaebelein (Ed.), *The Expositor's Bible Commentary: John and Acts* (Vol. 9, p. 136). Grand Rapids, MI: Zondervan Publishing House.
38. Keller, T. J. (2013). The Timothy Keller Sermon Archive. New York City: Redeemer Presbyterian Church.
39. Wiersbe, W. W. (1992). *Wiersbe's expository outlines on the New Testament* (p. 252). Wheaton, IL: Victor Books.
40. Keller, T. J. (2013). The Timothy Keller Sermon Archive. New York City: Redeemer Presbyterian Church.
41. Wiersbe, W. W. (1996). *The Bible exposition commentary* (Vol. 1, p. 360). Wheaton, IL: Victor Books.
42. https://www.worshiptogether.com/songs/holy-ground-beatty/
43. Barton, B. B. (1993). *John* (p. 336). Wheaton, IL: Tyndale House.
44. Barton, B. B. (1993). Ibid. (p. 343). Wheaton, IL: Tyndale House.
45. Wiersbe, W. W. (1996). *The Bible exposition commentary* (Vol. 1, p. 372). Wheaton, IL: Victor Books.
46. Barton, B. B. (1993). *John* (p. 361). Wheaton, IL: Tyndale House.
47. https://hymnary.org/text/i_hear_the_savior_say_thy_strength_indee
48. Barton, B. B. (1993). *John* (p. 362). Wheaton, IL: Tyndale House.
49. Barton, B. B. (1993). Ibid. (p. 365). Wheaton, IL: Tyndale House.
50. https://www.gotquestions.org/Jesus-sinless.html
51. Barton, B. B. (1993). *John* (p. 369). Wheaton, IL: Tyndale House.
52. Wiersbe, W. W. (1996). *The Bible exposition commentary* (Vol. 1, pp. 379–380). Wheaton, IL: Victor Books.
53. Wiersbe, W. W. (1996). Ibid. (Vol. 1, p. 381). Wheaton, IL: Victor Books.
54. Ken Gire. *Moments with the Savior*. Page 375
55. Wiersbe, W. W. (1992). *Wiersbe's expository outlines on the New Testament* (p. 266). Wheaton, IL: Victor Books.
56. Wiersbe, W. W. (1992). Ibid. (p. 266). Wheaton, IL: Victor Books.
57. Barton, B. B. (1993). *John* (p. 389). Wheaton, IL: Tyndale House.
58. Knowles, A. (2001). *The Bible guide* (1st Augsburg books ed., p. 529). Minneapolis, MN: Augsburg.
59. Boice, J. M. (2005). *The Gospel of John: an expositional commentary* (pp. 1583–1584). Grand Rapids, MI: Baker Books.
60. Tenney, M. C. (1981). John. In F. E. Gaebelein (Ed.), *The Expositor's Bible Commentary: John and Acts* (Vol. 9, p. 192). Grand Rapids, MI: Zondervan Publishing House.
61. Strobel, Lee. (1998). *The Case for Christ* (mass market paperback). Grand Rapids, MI: Zondervan Publishing House.
62. Boice, J. M. (2005). *The Gospel of John: an expositional commentary* (p. 1627). Grand Rapids, MI: Baker Books.